WORLD ATLAS

for
intermediate
students

Macmillan
McGraw-Hill

New York   Farmington

CONTENTS

THE WORLD

The earth is home to many different groups of people. People live in many different ways throughout the world, but we all share the same planet.

Imagine that you are an astronaut peering down at Planet Earth from your spaceship. What does the world look like from so high in the sky? One astronaut, Neil Armstrong, has said that from space the earth looks like a "tiny pea, pretty and blue."

From space the world's mountains, deserts, and other landforms look small and almost trivial. On the earth, however, they do much to shape the way we live. People all over the world use the land to meet their basic needs and wants. Because the

SPEED LIMIT
67,000 mph

The earth moves around the sun at a speed of 67,000 miles (106,200 km) per hour.

AROUND THE WORLD IN ...

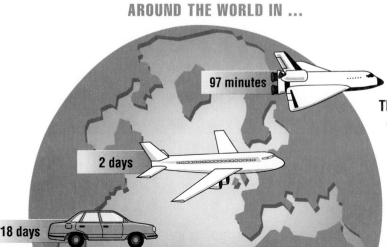

97 minutes

2 days

18 days

The earth is 24,000 miles (38,400 km) long at its center. A car can travel this distance in 18 days. According to the drawing, how long does it take a space shuttle to travel the same distance?

earth's landforms differ from place to place, people all over the world must work in different ways to meet their needs and wants.

As you look through this Atlas, or book of maps, keep in mind that no two places in the world are exactly alike. Think about what makes places throughout the world similar and different—things such as climate, landforms, and natural resources. Then think about how such things affect people and the way they live.

Oceans, mountains, deserts, and rain forests shape the way people live throughout the world.

Planet Earth looks like this from space.

According to the circle graph, how much of the earth is covered by water? Some of this water is contained in pretty lakes such as the one below.

THE EARTH

Salt Water 67%

Land 30%

Fresh Water 3%

THE WORLD
Physical

180°
160°W
140°W
120°W
100°W
80°W
60°W
80°N
ARCTIC OCEAN
ALASKA RANGE
Mt. McKinley
20,320 ft.
(6,194 m)
60°N
ROCKY MOUNTAINS
CANADIAN SHIELD
NORTH AMERICA
APPALACHIAN MTS.
Mississippi R.
40°N
NORTH PACIFIC OCEAN
Rio Grande
NORTH ATLANTIC OCEAN
Tropic of Cancer
20°N
0°
Equator
Amazon R.
ANDES MTS.
SOUTH AMERICA
20°S
Tropic of Capricorn
SOUTH PACIFIC OCEAN
Mt. Aconcagua
22,834 ft. (6,960 m)
40°S
Cape Horn
60°S
Antarctic Circle
Vinson Massif
16,864 ft. (5,140 m)
80°S
ANTARCTICA
180°

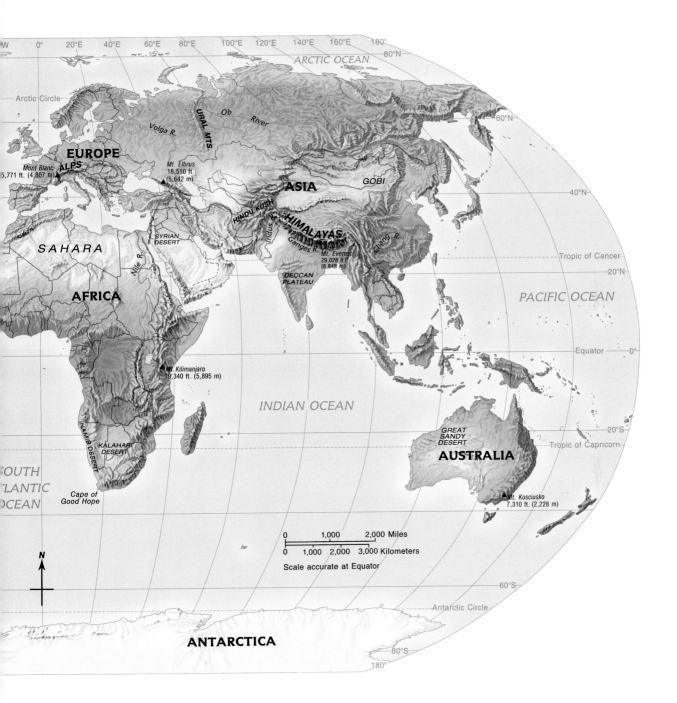

ARCTIC OCEAN

80°N

60°N

Arctic Circle

EUROPE

ALPS

Mont Blanc
5,771 ft. (4,807 m)

Volga R.

URAL MTS.

Ob

River

Mt. Elbrus
18,510 ft.
(5,642 m)

ASIA

GOBI

40°N

HINDU KUSH

SYRIAN
DESERT

HIMALAYAS

Indus R.

Ganges R.

Mt. Everest
29,028 ft.
(8,848 m)

Chang R.

SAHARA

Nile R.

DECCAN
PLATEAU

Tropic of Cancer

20°N

AFRICA

PACIFIC OCEAN

Equator

0°

Mt. Kilimanjaro
19,340 ft. (5,895 m)

INDIAN OCEAN

GREAT
SANDY
DESERT

20°S

NAMIB DESERT

KALAHARI
DESERT

AUSTRALIA

Tropic of Capricorn

SOUTH
ATLANTIC
OCEAN

Cape of
Good Hope

Mt. Kosciusko
7,310 ft. (2,228 m)

N

0   1,000   2,000 Miles

0   1,000   2,000   3,000 Kilometers

Scale accurate at Equator

60°S

Antarctic Circle

ANTARCTICA

80°S

180°

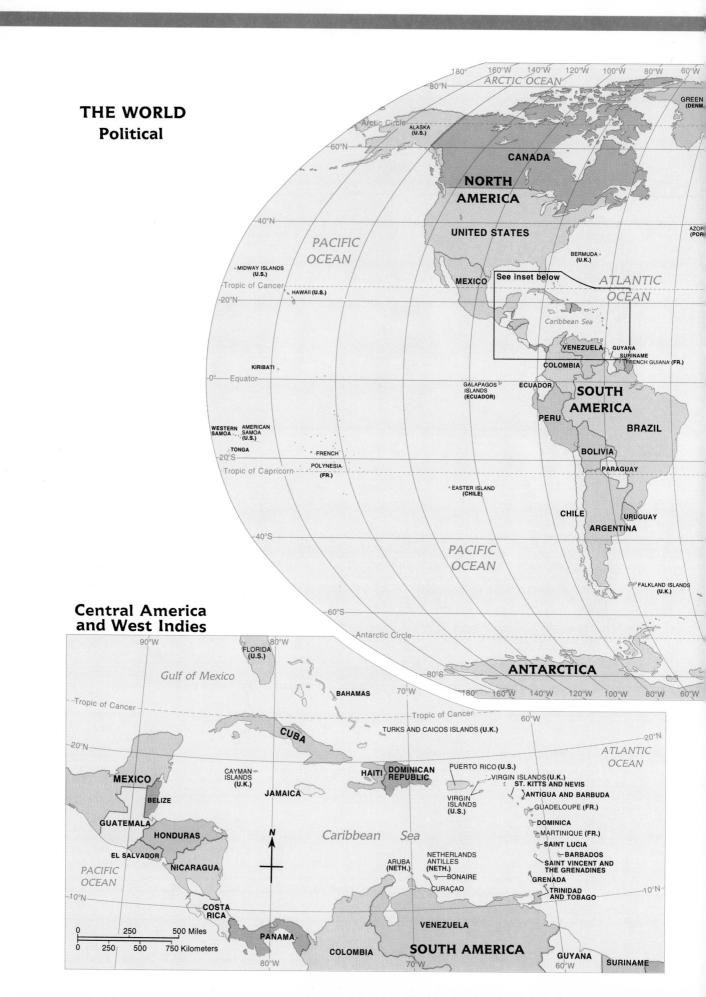

4

THE WORLD
Political

ARCTIC OCEAN

80°N

Arctic Circle

ALASKA (U.S.)

60°N

CANADA

NORTH AMERICA

GREEN. (DENM.

40°N

PACIFIC OCEAN

UNITED STATES

AZOR (POR

BERMUDA (U.K.)

MIDWAY ISLANDS (U.S.)

Tropic of Cancer

MEXICO

See inset below

ATLANTIC OCEAN

20°N

HAWAII (U.S.)

Caribbean Sea

VENEZUELA   GUYANA
SURINAME
COLOMBIA   FRENCH GUIANA (FR.)

KIRIBATI

0° Equator

GALAPAGOS ISLANDS (ECUADOR)

ECUADOR

SOUTH AMERICA

PERU

BRAZIL

WESTERN SAMOA   AMERICAN SAMOA (U.S.)

BOLIVIA

TONGA

FRENCH

PARAGUAY

20°S   POLYNESIA (FR.)

Tropic of Capricorn

EASTER ISLAND (CHILE)

CHILE   URUGUAY

ARGENTINA

40°S

PACIFIC OCEAN

FALKLAND ISLANDS (U.K.)

Central America and West Indies

60°S

Antarctic Circle

ANTARCTICA

80°S

180°   160°W   140°W   120°W   100°W   80°W   60°W

90°W

80°W

FLORIDA (U.S.)

Gulf of Mexico

BAHAMAS

70°W

Tropic of Cancer

Tropic of Cancer

60°W

20°N

CUBA

TURKS AND CAICOS ISLANDS (U.K.)

20°N

ATLANTIC OCEAN

MEXICO

CAYMAN ISLANDS (U.K.)

HAITI   DOMINICAN REPUBLIC

PUERTO RICO (U.S.)

VIRGIN ISLANDS (U.K.)
ST. KITTS AND NEVIS

BELIZE

JAMAICA

VIRGIN ISLANDS (U.S.)

ANTIGUA AND BARBUDA

GUADELOUPE (FR.)

GUATEMALA

N

DOMINICA

HONDURAS

Caribbean   Sea

MARTINIQUE (FR.)

SAINT LUCIA

EL SALVADOR

BARBADOS

NICARAGUA

NETHERLANDS ANTILLES (NETH.)

SAINT VINCENT AND THE GRENADINES

PACIFIC OCEAN

ARUBA (NETH.)

BONAIRE

GRENADA

TRINIDAD AND TOBAGO

10°N

CURAÇAO

10°N

COSTA RICA

VENEZUELA

0   250   500 Miles

PANAMA

0   250   500   750 Kilometers

COLOMBIA

SOUTH AMERICA

GUYANA

SURINAME

80°W

70°W

60°W

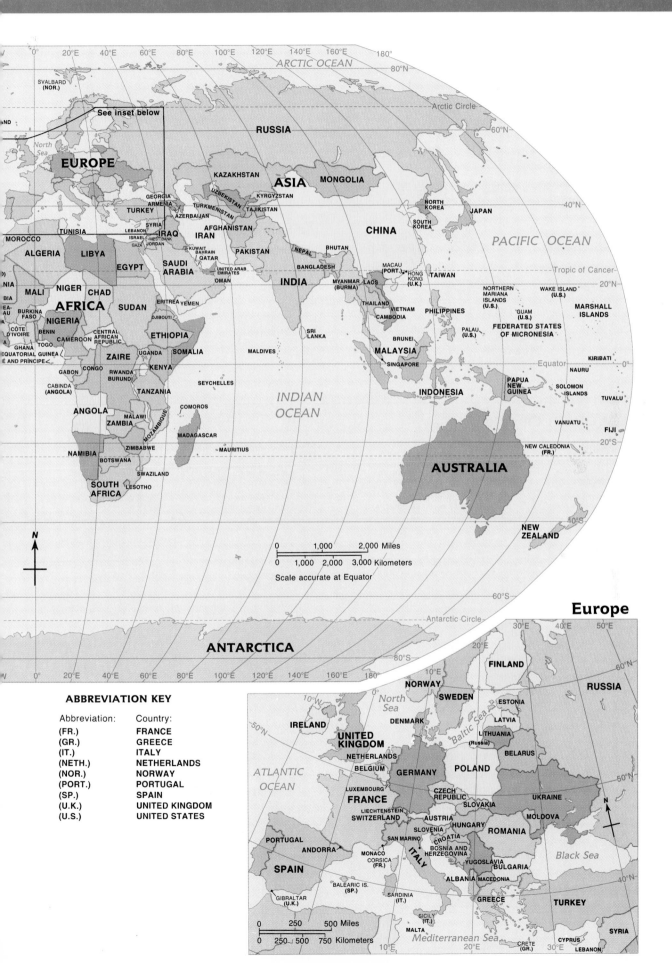

0° 20°E 40°E 60°E 80°E 100°E 120°E 140°E 160°E 180° 80°N

ARCTIC OCEAN

Arctic Circle

SVALBARD (NOR.)

See inset below

RUSSIA 60°N

North Sea

EUROPE

KAZAKHSTAN ASIA MONGOLIA

GEORGIA UZBEKISTAN KYRGYZSTAN 40°N

ARMENIA TURKMENISTAN TAJIKISTAN NORTH KOREA JAPAN

TURKEY AZERBAIJAN

SYRIA AFGHANISTAN CHINA SOUTH KOREA

TUNISIA LEBANON IRAQ IRAN PACIFIC OCEAN

ISRAEL WEST BANK PAKISTAN

MOROCCO GAZA JORDAN NEPAL BHUTAN

ALGERIA LIBYA KUWAIT MACAU (PORT.) Tropic of Cancer

EGYPT BAHRAIN QATAR BANGLADESH HONG KONG (U.K.) TAIWAN

SAUDI ARABIA UNITED ARAB EMIRATES 20°N

NIA MALI NIGER CHAD OMAN INDIA MYANMAR (BURMA) LAOS NORTHERN MARIANA ISLANDS (U.S.) WAKE ISLAND (U.S.)

BIA AFRICA SUDAN ERITREA YEMEN THAILAND VIETNAM MARSHALL ISLANDS

EA-AU BURKINA FASO DJIBOUTI CAMBODIA PHILIPPINES GUAM (U.S.)

NIGERIA CENTRAL AFRICAN REPUBLIC ETHIOPIA SRI LANKA PALAU (U.S.) FEDERATED STATES OF MICRONESIA

CÔTE D'IVOIRE BENIN CAMEROON MALDIVES BRUNEI

GHANA TOGO UGANDA SOMALIA MALAYSIA KIRIBATI

EQUATORIAL GUINEA ZAIRE KENYA SINGAPORE Equator NAURU 0°

É AND PRÍNCIPE GABON CONGO RWANDA BURUNDI SEYCHELLES INDONESIA PAPUA NEW GUINEA SOLOMON ISLANDS TUVALU

CABINDA (ANGOLA) TANZANIA INDIAN OCEAN COMOROS

ANGOLA MALAWI MADAGASCAR VANUATU 20°S

ZAMBIA MOZAMBIQUE MAURITIUS FIJI

NAMIBIA ZIMBABWE NEW CALEDONIA (FR.)

BOTSWANA AUSTRALIA

SWAZILAND

SOUTH AFRICA LESOTHO

N

0 1,000 2,000 Miles
0 1,000 2,000 3,000 Kilometers

Scale accurate at Equator

NEW ZEALAND 40°S

60°S

Antarctic Circle

ANTARCTICA 80°S

0° 20°E 40°E 60°E 80°E 100°E 120°E 140°E 160°E 180°

ABBREVIATION KEY

Abbreviation:	Country:
(FR.)	FRANCE
(GR.)	GREECE
(IT.)	ITALY
(NETH.)	NETHERLANDS
(NOR.)	NORWAY
(PORT.)	PORTUGAL
(SP.)	SPAIN
(U.K.)	UNITED KINGDOM
(U.S.)	UNITED STATES

Europe

30°E 40°E 50°E

FINLAND 60°N

NORWAY SWEDEN ESTONIA RUSSIA

North Sea DENMARK LATVIA

IRELAND Baltic Sea LITHUANIA

UNITED KINGDOM BELARUS

NETHERLANDS 50°N

BELGIUM GERMANY POLAND

ATLANTIC OCEAN LUXEMBOURG CZECH REPUBLIC UKRAINE

FRANCE SLOVAKIA

LIECHTENSTEIN AUSTRIA HUNGARY MOLDOVA

SWITZERLAND SLOVENIA ROMANIA

SAN MARINO CROATIA

PORTUGAL MONACO BOSNIA AND HERZEGOVINA Black Sea

ANDORRA CORSICA (FR.) ITALY YUGOSLAVIA BULGARIA 40°N

SPAIN ALBANIA MACEDONIA

BALEARIC IS. (SP.) SARDINIA (IT.) GREECE TURKEY

GIBRALTAR (U.K.) SICILY (IT.)

0 250 500 Miles MALTA Mediterranean Sea CRETE (GR.) CYPRUS SYRIA

0 250 500 750 Kilometers 10°E 20°E 30°E LEBANON

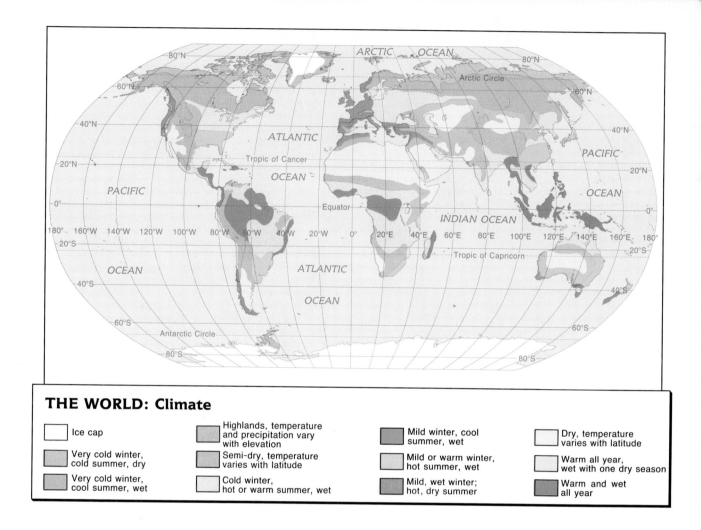

THE WORLD: Climate

☐	Ice cap
☐	Very cold winter, cold summer, dry
☐	Very cold winter, cool summer, wet
☐	Highlands, temperature and precipitation vary with elevation
☐	Semi-dry, temperature varies with latitude
☐	Cold winter, hot or warm summer, wet
☐	Mild winter, cool summer, wet
☐	Mild or warm winter, hot summer, wet
☐	Mild, wet winter; hot, dry summer
☐	Dry, temperature varies with latitude
☐	Warm all year, wet with one dry season
☐	Warm and wet all year

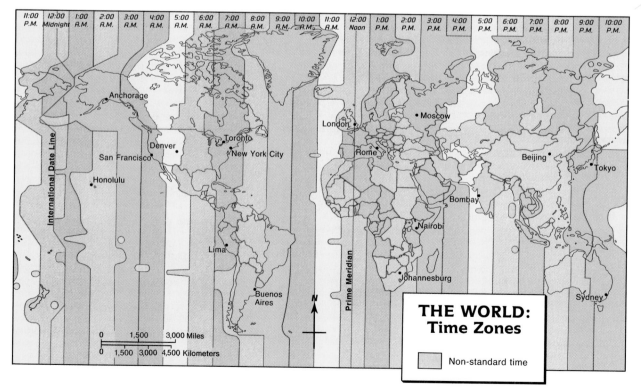

THE WORLD: Time Zones

☐ Non-standard time

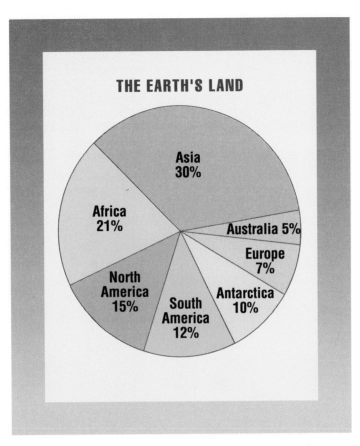

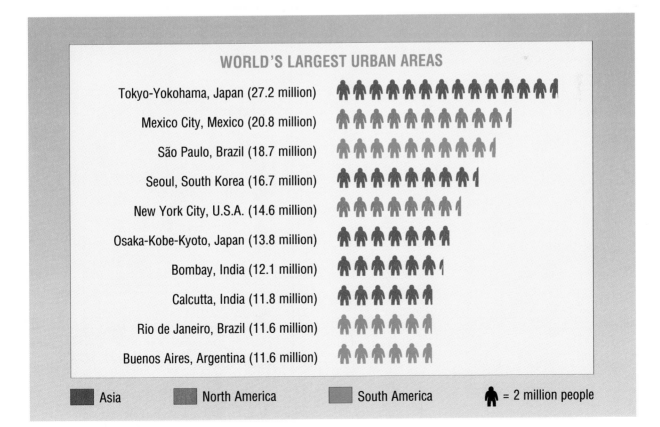

8

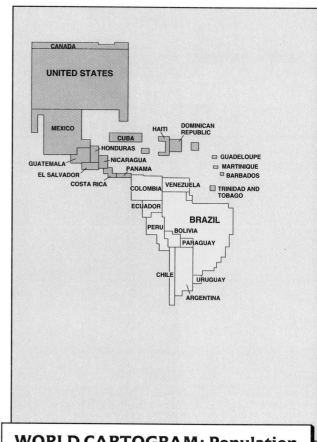

WORLD CARTOGRAM: Population

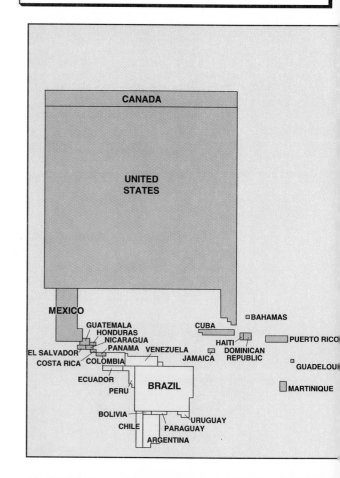

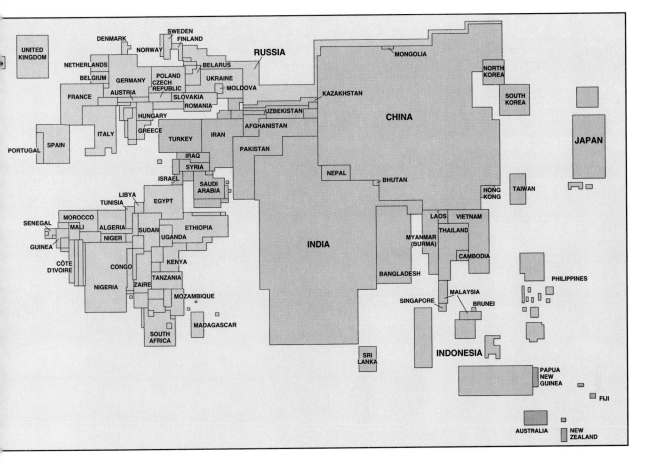

WORLD CARTOGRAM: Gross National Product

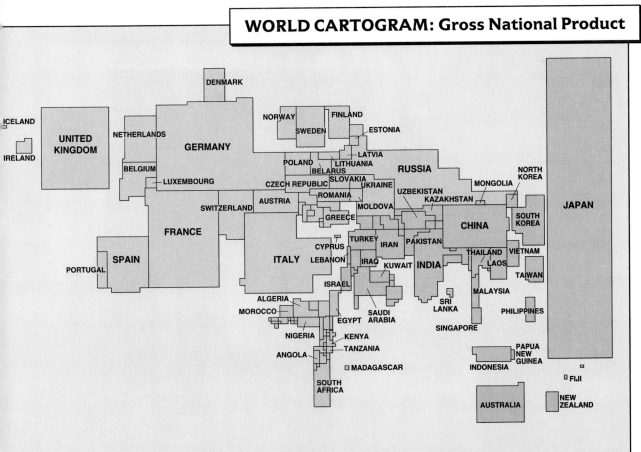

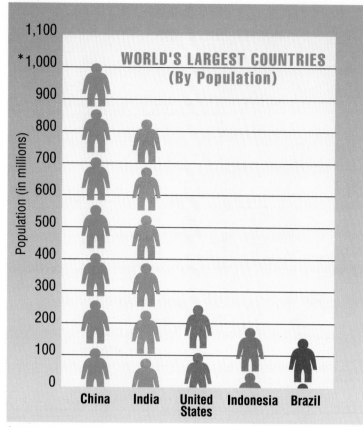

* 1,000 million = 1 billion

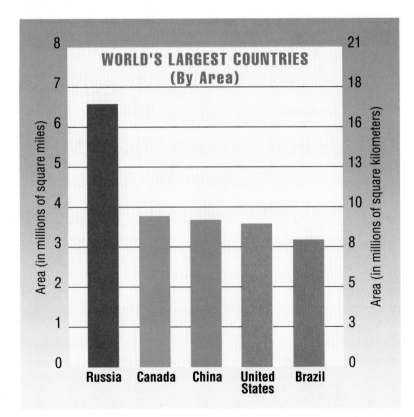

LONGEST RIVERS OF THE WORLD

River	Country	Length in miles (kilometers)
Nile	Egypt	4,100 miles (6,560 km)
Amazon	Brazil	4,000 miles (6,400 km)
Chang Jiang (Yangtze)	China	3,964 miles (6,342 km)
Mississippi-Missouri	United States	3,710 miles (5,936 km)
Ob	Russia	3,362 miles (5,379 km)
Huang (Yellow)	China	2,903 miles (4,644 km)
Congo	Zaire	2,900 miles (4,640 km)
Amur	Russia	2,744 miles (4,390 km)
Lena	Russia	2,734 miles (4,374 km)
Mackenzie	Canada	2,635 miles (4,216 km)
Mekong	China	2,600 miles (4,160 km)
Yenisey	Russia	2,543 miles (4,068 km)

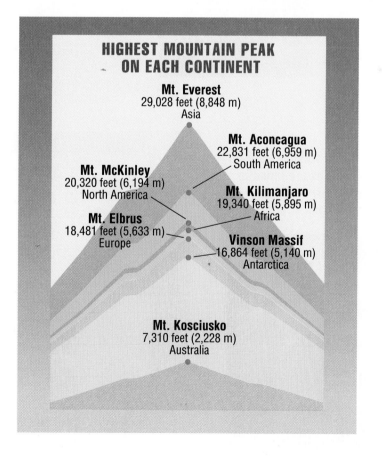

HIGHEST MOUNTAIN PEAK ON EACH CONTINENT

Mt. Everest 29,028 feet (8,848 m) Asia

Mt. Aconcagua 22,831 feet (6,959 m) South America

Mt. McKinley 20,320 feet (6,194 m) North America

Mt. Kilimanjaro 19,340 feet (5,895 m) Africa

Mt. Elbrus 18,481 feet (5,633 m) Europe

Vinson Massif 16,864 feet (5,140 m) Antarctica

Mt. Kosciusko 7,310 feet (2,228 m) Australia

UNITED STATES AND CANADA

Much of the continent of North America consists of just two countries, the United States and Canada. These countries share many things in common: mountain ranges, grassy plains, the Great Lakes, and the longest unguarded border in the world. In both countries English is the principal language.

There are also many differences between the United States and Canada. The United States has almost ten times as many people as Canada,

People of many different backgrounds live in the countries of the United States and Canada.

Vast plains and towering mountains are found in both the United States and Canada.

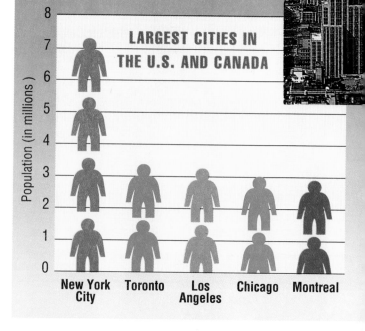

LARGEST CITIES IN THE U.S. AND CANADA

Population (in millions)

8				
7				
6				
5				
4				
3				
2				
1				
0				
New York City	Toronto	Los Angeles	Chicago	Montreal

although Canada is a larger country. French is spoken in some areas of Canada. Forests cover much of Canada, whereas most forests in the United States have been cleared to make way for towns and cities. Canada's most important exports are forest products. In contrast, the most important exports of the United States are machinery and transportation equipment.

Take a close look at the maps of this region. Find as many differences as you can between the landforms that make up Canada and the United States. Then find as many similarities as you can between the two countries. Identify some of the common features of this region.

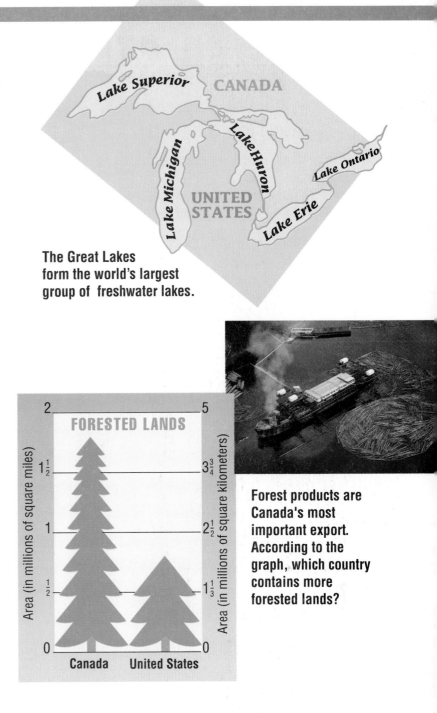

The Great Lakes form the world's largest group of freshwater lakes.

Forest products are Canada's most important export. According to the graph, which country contains more forested lands?

New York City (*left*) is the largest city in this region. According to the graph, what is the population of Toronto (*below*)?

Both Canada and the United States have thousands of miles of beautiful coastland.

14

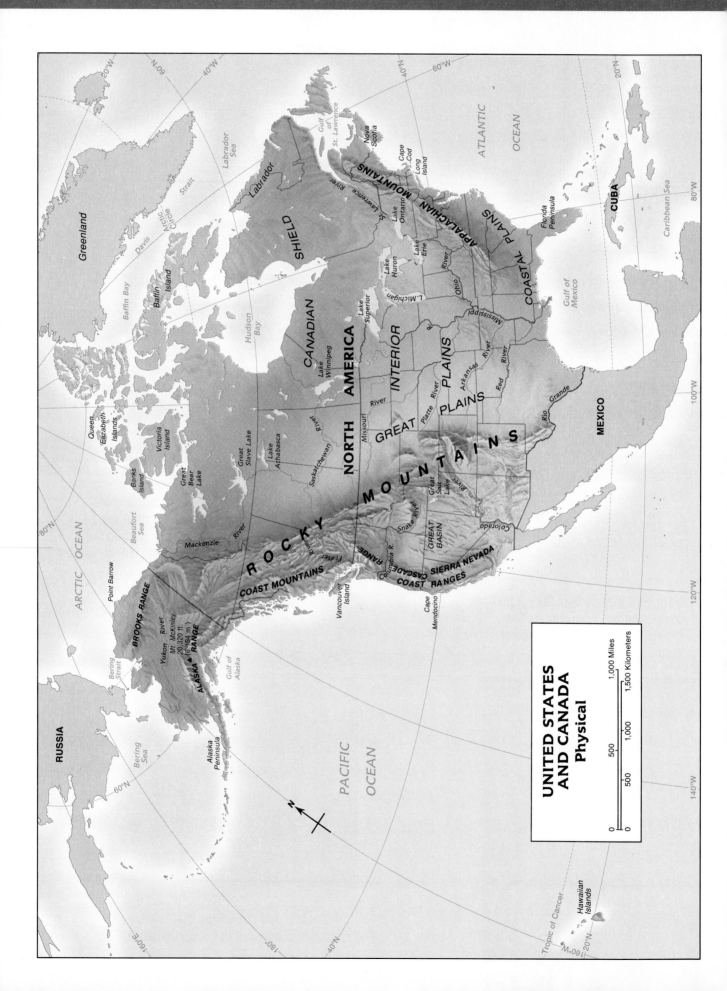

UNITED STATES
AND CANADA
Physical

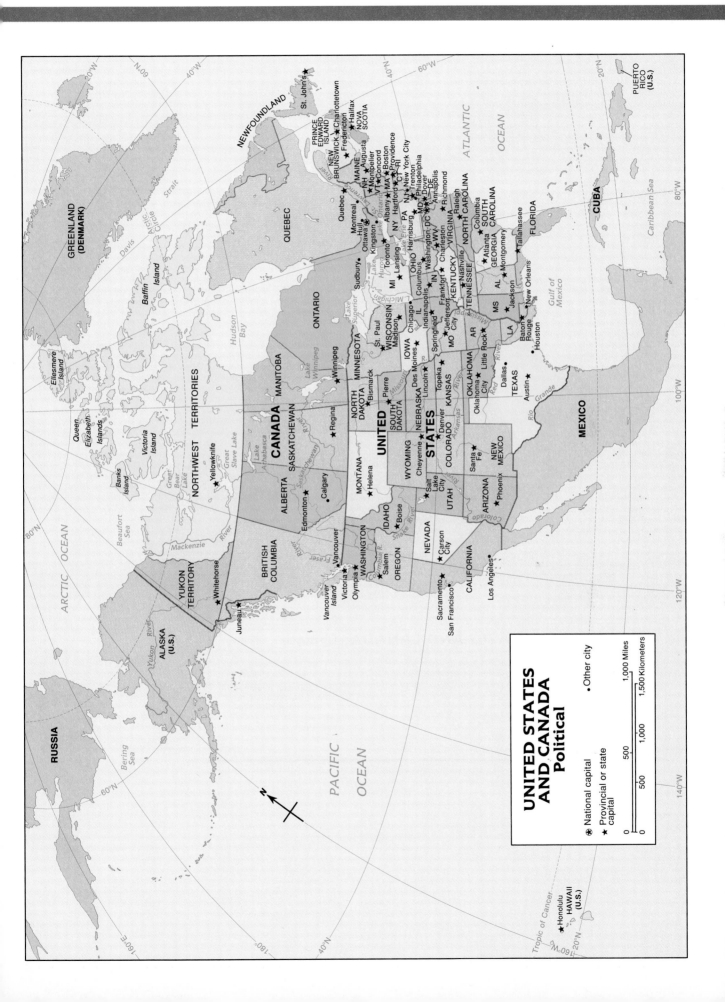

UNITED STATES
AND CANADA
Political

⊕ National capital • Other city
★ Provincial or state
  capital

0   500   1,000 Miles
0   500   1,000   1,500 Kilometers

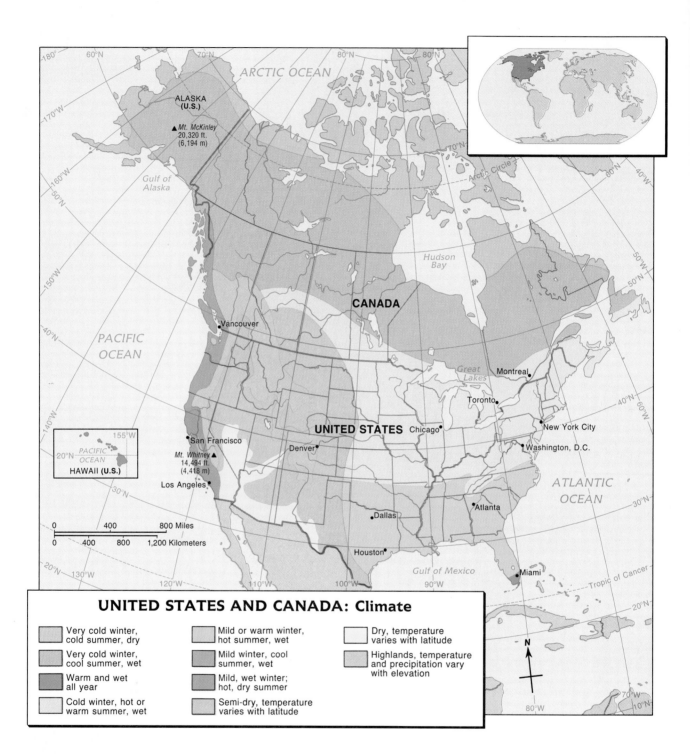

UNITED STATES AND CANADA: Climate

- Very cold winter, cold summer, dry
- Very cold winter, cool summer, wet
- Warm and wet all year
- Cold winter, hot or warm summer, wet
- Mild or warm winter, hot summer, wet
- Mild winter, cool summer, wet
- Mild, wet winter; hot, dry summer
- Semi-dry, temperature varies with latitude
- Dry, temperature varies with latitude
- Highlands, temperature and precipitation vary with elevation

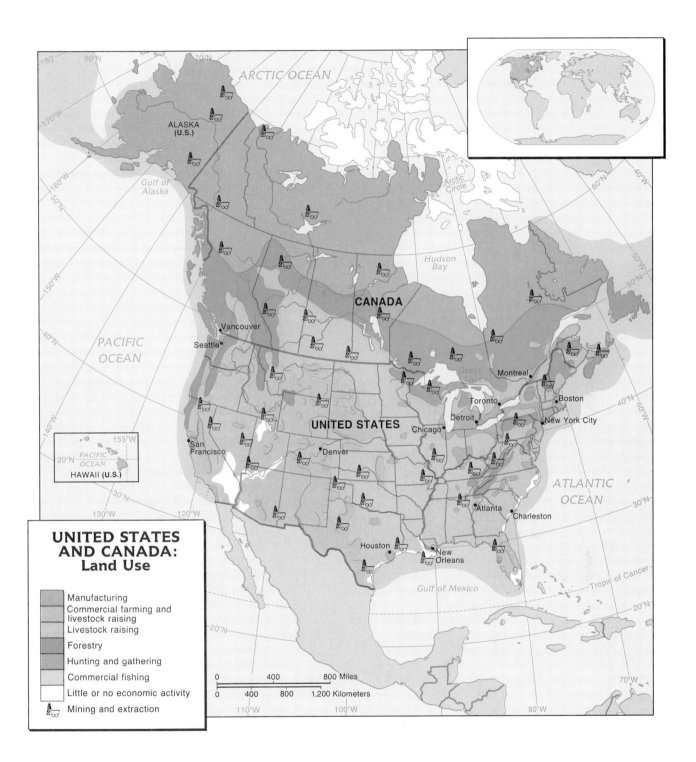

UNITED STATES
AND CANADA:
Land Use

Manufacturing
Commercial farming and
livestock raising
Livestock raising
Forestry
Hunting and gathering
Commercial fishing
Little or no economic activity
Mining and extraction

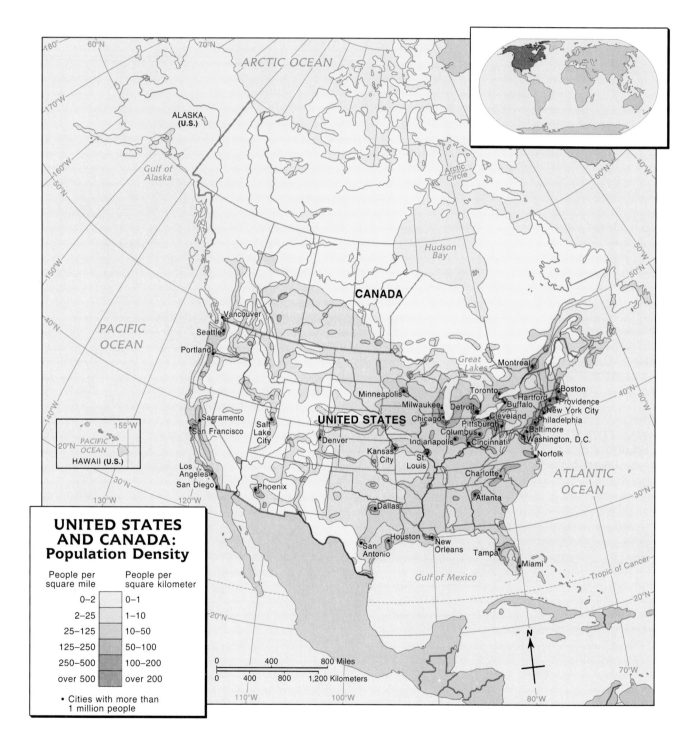

UNITED STATES AND CANADA: Population Density

People per square mile	People per square kilometer
0–2	0–1
2–25	1–10
25–125	10–50
125–250	50–100
250–500	100–200
over 500	over 200

• Cities with more than 1 million people

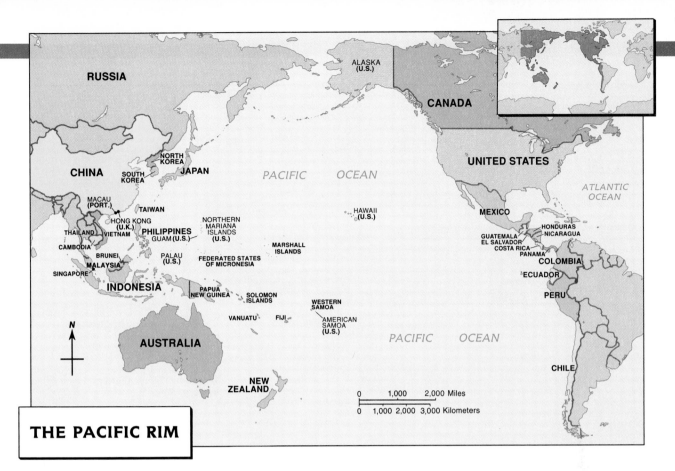

RUSSIA

ALASKA (U.S.)

CANADA

CHINA
NORTH KOREA
SOUTH KOREA
JAPAN

PACIFIC OCEAN

UNITED STATES

MACAU (PORT.)
TAIWAN
HONG KONG (U.K.)
THAILAND
VIETNAM
PHILIPPINES
GUAM (U.S.)
CAMBODIA
NORTHERN MARIANA ISLANDS (U.S.)
HAWAII (U.S.)

ATLANTIC OCEAN

MEXICO

GUATEMALA
EL SALVADOR
COSTA RICA
HONDURAS
NICARAGUA
PANAMA
COLOMBIA

BRUNEI
MALAYSIA
PALAU (U.S.)
FEDERATED STATES OF MICRONESIA
MARSHALL ISLANDS

ECUADOR

SINGAPORE
INDONESIA
PAPUA NEW GUINEA
SOLOMON ISLANDS
WESTERN SAMOA
PERU

N

VANUATU
FIJI
AMERICAN SAMOA (U.S.)

PACIFIC OCEAN

AUSTRALIA

NEW ZEALAND

0 1,000 2,000 Miles
0 1,000 2,000 3,000 Kilometers

CHILE

THE PACIFIC RIM

CANADA AND THE UNITED STATES

	Canada	United States
Area	3,851,798 sq mi; 9,976,140 sq km	3,623,420 sq mi; 9,384,658 sq km
Population	26,800,000	252,800,000
People per square mile	7	70
Gross national product	$572 billion	$5,686 billion
Leading exports	Forest products	Machinery and transportation equipment
Most important trading partner	United States	Canada
Capital	Ottawa	Washington, D.C.

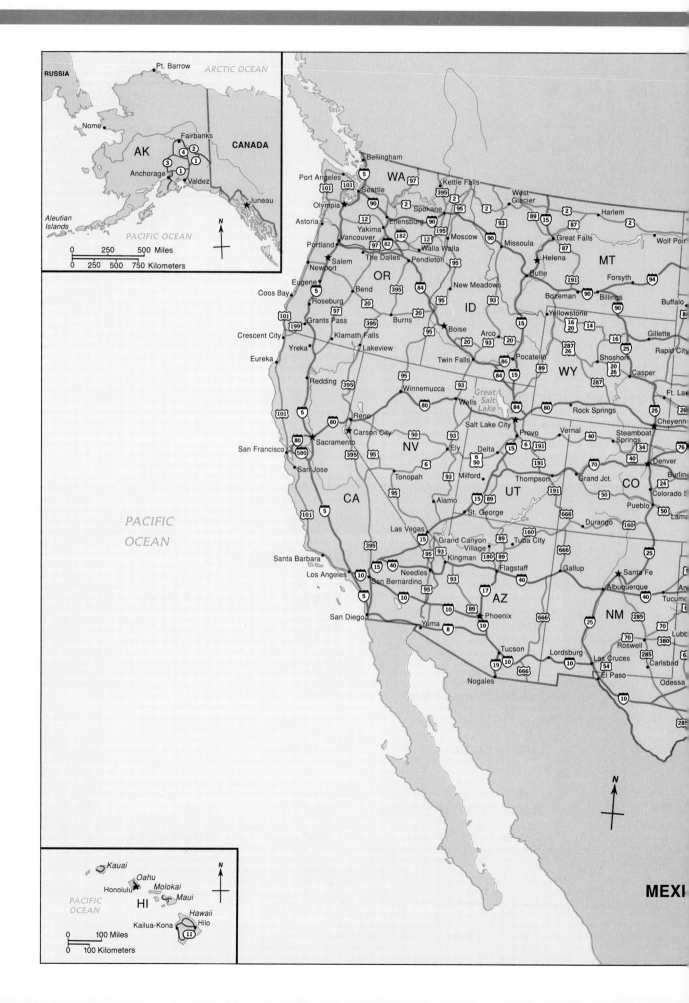

RUSSIA

ARCTIC OCEAN

Pt. Barrow

Nome

AK

Fairbanks

④ ②

③ ①

①

Anchorage

Valdez

CANADA

Juneau

Aleutian Islands

PACIFIC OCEAN

0   250   500 Miles

0   250   500   750 Kilometers

N

Bellingham

Port Angeles

⑤

Seattle

WA

Kettle Falls

⑨⑦

③⑨⑤

②

West Glacier

⑧⑨

②

Harlem

②

Olympia

①⓪①

Astoria

⑫

Yakima

Ellensburg

⑨⓪

Spokane

⑨⑤

②

⑧⑨

①⑤

②

⑧⑦

Great Falls

Wolf Poin

Portland

Vancouver

⑨⑦

⑧②

①⑧②

⑫

Walla Walla

Moscow

⑨⓪

Missoula

Helena

⑧⑦

MT

Newport

Salem

The Dalles

Pendleton

⑨⑤

Butte

①⑨①

Forsyth

⑨④

Eugene

OR

Bend

③⑨⑤

⑧④

New Meadows

Bozeman

⑨⓪

Billings

⑤

Coos Bay

⑤

Roseburg

⑨⑦

⑳

Burns

⑳

⑨⑤

ID

⑨③

Yellowstone

①⑥ ⑳

①④

Buffalo

Gillette

Grants Pass

①⑨⑨

③⑨⑤

⑨⑤

Boise

Arco

⑳

⑳

②⑧⑦ ②⑥

①⑥

②⑤

Rapid City

Crescent City

Klamath Falls

Twin Falls

⑧⑥

Pocatello

⑳ ②⑥

Shoshon

Casper

Eureka

Yreka

Lakeview

⑨③

⑧④

①⑤

⑧⑨

WY

②⑧⑦

Ft. La

Redding

③⑨⑤

⑨⑤

Winnemucca

⑨③

Great Salt Lake

Wells

⑧④

⑧⓪

Rock Springs

②⑤

Cheyenn

⑤

⑧⓪

Reno

⑧⓪

Carson City

Sacramento

⑤⑧⓪

San Francisco

③⑨⑤

⑨⑤

⑤⓪

NV

⑨③

Ely

Salt Lake City

Provo

Vernal

④⓪

Steamboat Springs

③④

⑦⑥

San Jose

⑥

Delta

⑥

①⑤

⑥

①⑨①

⑦⓪

④⓪

Denver

Burlin

Tonopah

⑨③

Milford

Thompson

Grand Jct.

①⑨①

⑤⓪

CO

②④

CA

⑨⑤

Alamo

①⑤

⑧⑨

UT

①⑨①

Pueblo

⑤⓪

Lama

St. George

⑥⑥⑥

Durango

①⑥⓪

①⓪①

⑤

Las Vegas

⑧⑨

①⑥⓪

Tuba City

⑥⑥⑥

②⑤

Santa Barbara

③⑨⑤

⑨

Grand Canyon Village

⑧⑨

Kingman

⑨⑤

⑨③

①⑧⓪

⑧⑨

Flagstaff

Gallup

Santa Fe

Los Angeles

⑤

①⑤

④⓪

Needles

San Bernardino

⑩

①⓪

⑨③

AZ

①⑦

④⓪

Albuquerque

An

Tucumc

⑤

①⓪

⑨⑤

①⓪

⑧⑨

Phoenix

⑥⑥⑥

②⑤

NM

②⑧⑤

④⓪

⑦⓪

San Diego

Yuma

①⓪

①⓪

Tucson

Lordsburg

Las Cruces

②⑧⑤

⑦⓪

③⑧⓪

Lubb

Roswell

⑧

①⑨

①⓪

Nogales

⑥⑥⑥

①⓪

⑤④

El Paso

Carlsbad

Odessa

①⓪

②⑧⑤

PACIFIC OCEAN

N

Kauai

Oahu

Molokai

Honolulu

Maui

HI

PACIFIC OCEAN

Hawaii

Kailua-Kona

Hilo

⑪

0   100 Miles

0   100 Kilometers

N

MEXI

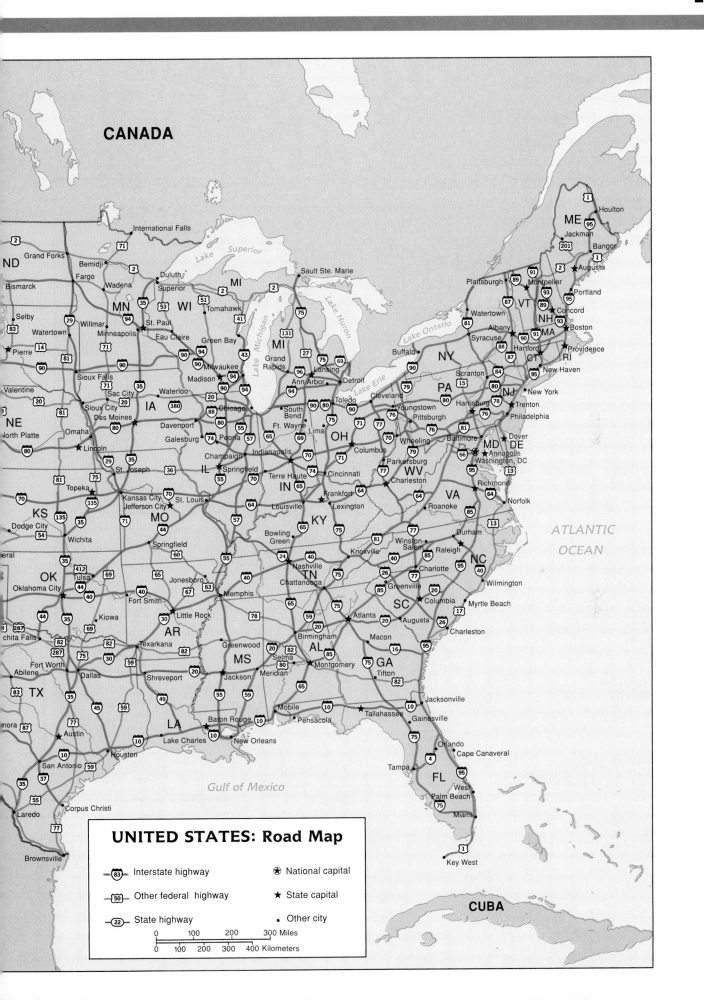

CANADA

UNITED STATES: Road Map

- 🛡83 Interstate highway
- 🛡50 Other federal highway
- 🛡22 State highway

- ✪ National capital
- ★ State capital
- • Other city

| 0 | 100 | 200 | 300 Miles |
| 0 | 100 | 200 | 300 | 400 Kilometers |

CUBA

ATLANTIC OCEAN

Gulf of Mexico

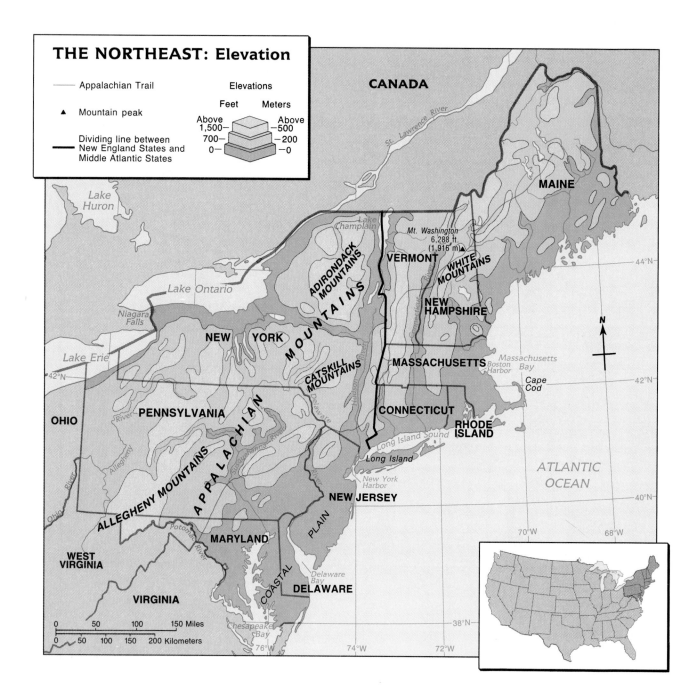

THE NORTHEAST: Elevation

— Appalachian Trail

▲ Mountain peak

▬ Dividing line between New England States and Middle Atlantic States

Elevations

Feet	Meters
Above 1,500—	Above —500
700—	—200
0—	—0

CANADA

St. Lawrence River

MAINE

Lake Huron

Lake Ontario

Lake Champlain

ADIRONDACK MOUNTAINS

MOUNTAINS

VERMONT

WHITE MOUNTAINS

Mt. Washington 6,288 ft. (1,916 m)▲

NEW HAMPSHIRE

Niagara Falls

NEW   YORK

Lake Erie

42°N

CATSKILL MOUNTAINS

Hudson River

MASSACHUSETTS

Boston Harbor

Massachusetts Bay

Cape Cod

42°N

44°N

OHIO

PENNSYLVANIA

River

Allegheny

Delaware River

Susquehanna River

CONNECTICUT

RHODE ISLAND

Long Island Sound

APPALACHIAN

ALLEGHENY MOUNTAINS

Long Island

New York Harbor

ATLANTIC OCEAN

NEW JERSEY

40°N

Ohio River

WEST VIRGINIA

MARYLAND

Potomac River

COASTAL PLAIN

DELAWARE

Delaware Bay

70°W

68°W

VIRGINIA

Chesapeake Bay

38°N

76°W   74°W   72°W

N

0   50   100   150 Miles

0   50   100   150   200 Kilometers

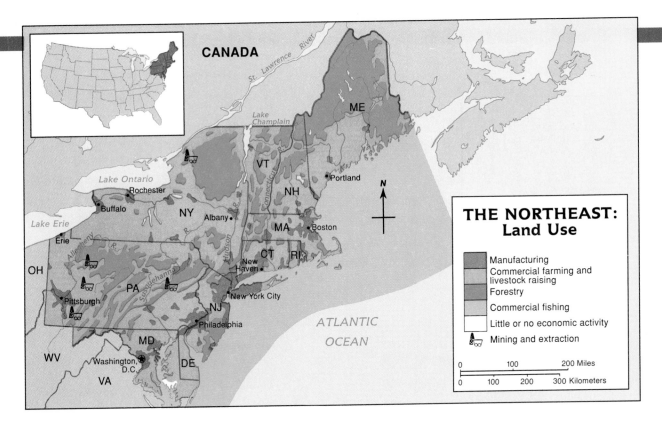

CANADA

St. Lawrence River

Lake Champlain

Lake Ontario

Rochester

Buffalo

Lake Erie

Erie

OH

Allegheny R.

Pittsburgh

PA

Susquehanna R.

NJ

MD

WV

Washington, D.C.

DE

VA

NY

Albany

Hudson R.

Connecticut R.

VT

NH

Portland

ME

MA

Boston

CT

RI

New Haven

New York City

Philadelphia

ATLANTIC OCEAN

N

THE NORTHEAST: Land Use

- Manufacturing
- Commercial farming and livestock raising
- Forestry
- Commercial fishing
- Little or no economic activity
- Mining and extraction

0   100   200 Miles

0   100   200   300 Kilometers

STATES OF THE NORTHEAST

State	Capital	Population	Area in sq mi (sq km)	Date of Statehood
Connecticut	Hartford	3,287,116	5,544 (14,358)	1788
Delaware	Dover	666,168	2,489 (6,446)	1787
Maine	Augusta	1,227,928	35,387 (91,652)	1820
Maryland	Annapolis	4,781,468	12,407 (32,134)	1788
Massachusetts	Boston	6,016,425	10,555 (27,337)	1788
New Hampshire	Concord	1,109,252	9,351 (24,219)	1788
New Jersey	Trenton	7,730,188	8,722 (22,590)	1787
New York	Albany	17,990,455	54,475 (141,090)	1788
Pennsylvania	Harrisburg	11,881,643	46,058 (119,290)	1787
Rhode Island	Providence	1,003,464	1,545 (4,002)	1790
Vermont	Montpelier	562,758	9,615 (24,903)	1791

Population figures: 1990 Census

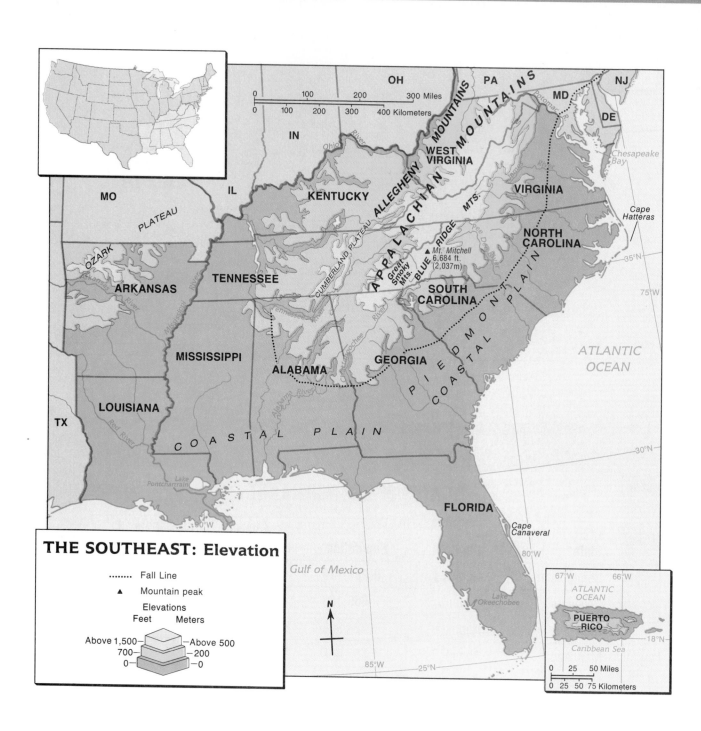

THE SOUTHEAST: Elevation

.... Fall Line

▲ Mountain peak

Elevations

Feet | Meters

Above 1,500 — Above 500
700 — 200
0 — 0

OH

PA

NJ

MD

DE

IN

Ohio River

WEST VIRGINIA

ALLEGHENY MOUNTAINS

APPALACHIAN MOUNTAINS

VIRGINIA

MO

PLATEAU

KENTUCKY

Chesapeake Bay

Cape Hatteras

IL

CUMBERLAND PLATEAU

▲ Mt. Mitchell
6,684 ft.
(2,037m)

NORTH CAROLINA

35°N

75°W

OZARK

ARKANSAS

TENNESSEE

Arkansas River

Mississippi River

Tennessee River

Great Smoky Mts.

BLUE RIDGE MTS.

Pee Dee River

SOUTH CAROLINA

PIEDMONT

COASTAL PLAIN

MISSISSIPPI

ALABAMA

GEORGIA

Alabama River

Chattahoochee River

LOUISIANA

Red River

TX

C O A S T A L   P L A I N

Lake Pontchartrain

90°W

Gulf of Mexico

ATLANTIC OCEAN

FLORIDA

Cape Canaveral

80°W

Lake Okeechobee

30°N

N

85°W

25°N

67°W 66°W

ATLANTIC OCEAN

PUERTO RICO

Caribbean Sea

18°N

0   25   50 Miles
0 25 50 75 Kilometers

0   100   200   300 Miles
0   100   200   300   400 Kilometers

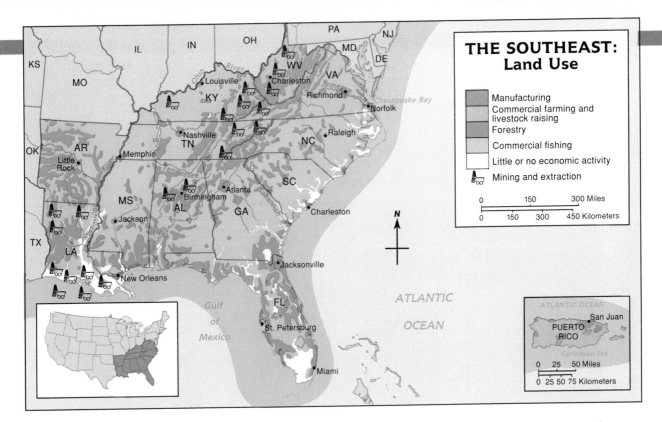

THE SOUTHEAST:
Land Use

Manufacturing
Commercial farming and livestock raising
Forestry
Commercial fishing
Little or no economic activity
Mining and extraction

STATES OF THE SOUTHEAST

State	Capital	Population	Area in sq mi (sq km)	Date of Statehood
Alabama	Montgomery	4,040,587	52,423 (135,776)	1819
Arkansas	Little Rock	2,350,725	53,182 (137,741)	1836
Florida	Tallahassee	12,937,926	65,758 (170,314)	1845
Georgia	Atlanta	6,478,216	59,441 (153,952)	1788
Kentucky	Frankfort	3,685,296	40,411 (104,664)	1792
Louisiana	Baton Rouge	4,219,000	51,843 (134,273)	1812
Mississippi	Jackson	2,573,216	48,434 (125,444)	1817
North Carolina	Raleigh	6,628,637	53,821 (139,396)	1789
South Carolina	Columbia	3,486,703	32,007 (82,898)	1788
Tennessee	Nashville	4,877,185	42,146 (109,158)	1796
Virginia	Richmond	6,187,358	42,769 (110,772)	1788
West Virginia	Charleston	1,793,477	24,231 (65,758)	1863

Population figures: 1990 Census

THE MIDDLE WEST: Elevation

Elevations

Feet	Meters
Above 1,500	Above 500
700	200
0	0

▲ Mountain peak

— Dividing line between Great Lakes States and Plains States

MT

GREAT PLAINS

NORTH DAKOTA

Lake Sakakawea

MINNESOTA

MESABI RANGE

Lake of the Woods

Lake Superior

CANADA

MICHIGAN

BLACK HILLS
▲ Harney Peak
7,242 ft.
(2,207 m)

Lake Oahe

SOUTH DAKOTA

WISCONSIN

Mississippi River

Wisconsin River

Lake Huron

Lake Michigan

Lake Ontario

WY

NEBRASKA

INTERIOR PLAINS

Des Moines River

IOWA

CENTRAL

Mississippi River

Illinois River

ILLINOIS

INDIANA

Wabash River

OHIO

Lake Erie

PA

Platte River

Missouri River

PLAINS

PLAINS

WEST VIRGINIA

COLORADO

KANSAS

Arkansas River

Missouri River

Ohio River

MISSOURI

OZARK PLATEAU

KENTUCKY

VIRGINIA

NM

OKLAHOMA

TEXAS

ARKANSAS

N

MS

TENNESSEE

NC

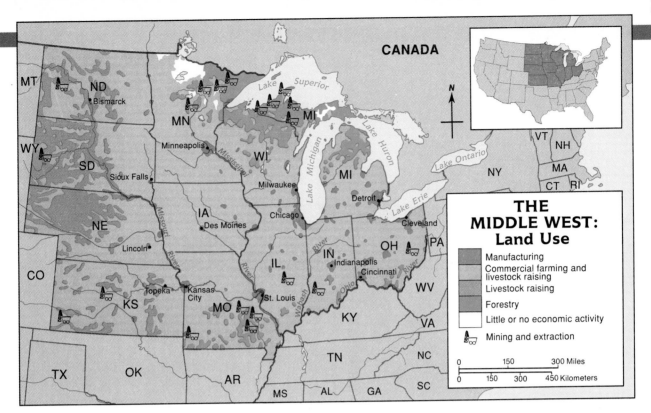

STATES OF THE MIDDLE WEST

State	Capital	Population	Area in sq mi (sq km)	Date of Statehood
Illinois	Springfield	11,430,602	57,918 (150,008)	1818
Indiana	Indianapolis	5,544,159	36,420 (94,328)	1816
Iowa	Des Moines	2,776,755	56,276 (145,755)	1846
Kansas	Topeka	2,477,574	82,282 (213,110)	1861
Michigan	Lansing	9,295,297	96,810 (250,738)	1837
Minnesota	St. Paul	4,375,099	86,943 (225,182)	1858
Missouri	Jefferson City	5,117,073	69,709 (180,546)	1821
Nebraska	Lincoln	1,578,385	77,358 (200,357)	1867
North Dakota	Bismarck	638,800	70,704 (183,123)	1889
Ohio	Columbus	10,847,115	44,828 (116,105)	1803
South Dakota	Pierre	696,004	77,121 (199,743)	1889
Wisconsin	Madison	4,891,769	65,503 (169,653)	1848

Population figures: 1990 Census

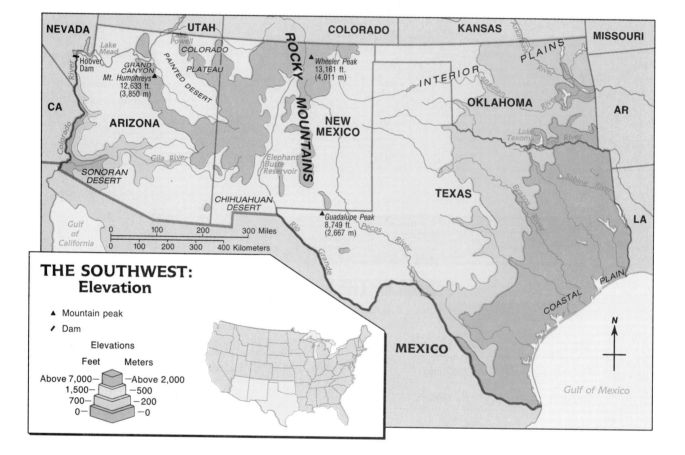

THE SOUTHWEST: Elevation

- ▲ Mountain peak
- ✐ Dam

Elevations

Feet	Meters
Above 7,000—	—Above 2,000
1,500—	—500
700—	—200
0—	—0

NEVADA
UTAH
COLORADO
KANSAS
MISSOURI
Lake Powell
COLORADO PLATEAU
Lake Mead
Hoover Dam
GRAND CANYON
Mt. Humphreys 12,633 ft. (3,850 m)
PAINTED DESERT
ROCKY MOUNTAINS
Wheeler Peak 13,161 ft. (4,011 m)
INTERIOR
PLAINS
Arkansas River
Canadian River
CA
ARIZONA
Colorado River
Gila River
NEW MEXICO
OKLAHOMA
AR
Lake Texoma
Red River
SONORAN DESERT
Elephant Butte Reservoir
CHIHUAHUAN DESERT
TEXAS
Brazos River
Sabine River
Gulf of California
Guadalupe Peak 8,749 ft. (2,667 m)
Rio Grande
Pecos River
LA
MEXICO
COASTAL PLAIN
Gulf of Mexico

0	100	200	300 Miles
0	100	200	300	400 Kilometers

N

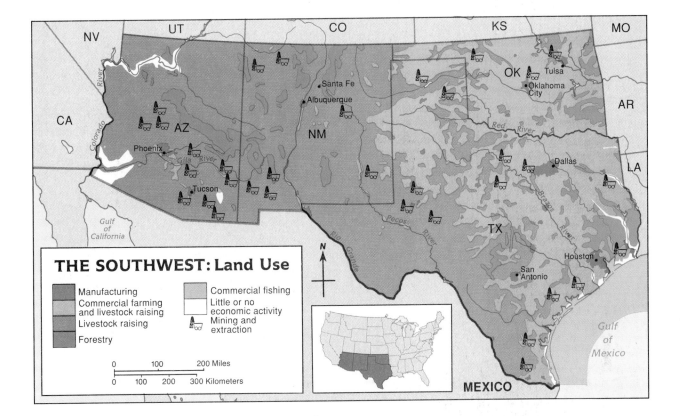

THE SOUTHWEST: Land Use

Manufacturing

Commercial farming and livestock raising

Livestock raising

Forestry

Commercial fishing

Little or no economic activity

Mining and extraction

0   100   200 Miles

0   100   200   300 Kilometers

NV UT CO KS MO
CA AZ NM OK AR LA
TX MEXICO

Santa Fe
Albuquerque
Phoenix
Gila River
Tucson
Gulf of California
Colorado River
Rio Grande
Pecos River
Red River
Brazos River
Tulsa
Oklahoma City
Dallas
Houston
San Antonio
Gulf of Mexico

STATES OF THE SOUTHWEST

State	Capital	Population	Area in sq mi (sq km)	Date of Statehood
Arizona	Phoenix	3,665,228	114,006 (295,276)	1912
New Mexico	Santa Fe	1,515,069	121,598 (314,938)	1912
Oklahoma	Oklahoma City	3,145,585	69,903 (181,049)	1907
Texas	Austin	16,986,510	268,601 (695,677)	1845

Population figures: 1990 Census

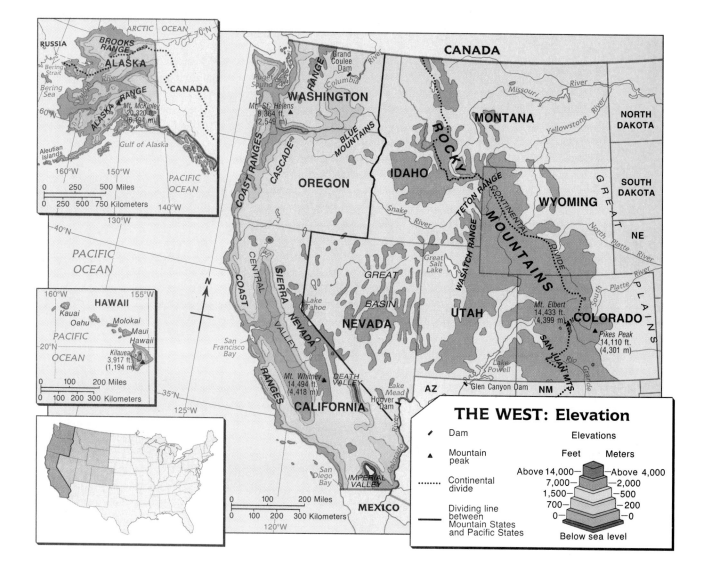

ARCTIC OCEAN
75°N

RUSSIA
BROOKS RANGE
ALASKA
Bering Strait
Bering Sea
River
ALASKA RANGE
Mt. McKinley 20,320 ft. (6,194 m)
Aleutian Islands
Gulf of Alaska
60°N
CANADA
160°W   150°W
PACIFIC OCEAN
0   250   500 Miles
0 250 500 750 Kilometers   140°W
130°W

40°N

PACIFIC OCEAN

HAWAII
160°W   155°W
Kauai
Oahu
Molokai
Maui
Hawaii
PACIFIC OCEAN
20°N
Kilauea 3,917 ft. (1,194 m)
0   100   200 Miles
0 100 200 300 Kilometers
35°N
125°W
120°W

N

CANADA

Grand Coulee Dam
Columbia River
WASHINGTON
Mt. St. Helens 8,364 ft. (2,549 m)
Puget Sound
CASCADE RANGE
COAST RANGES
BLUE MOUNTAINS
OREGON
IDAHO
Snake River
ROCKY
MONTANA
Missouri River
Yellowstone River
NORTH DAKOTA
SOUTH DAKOTA
WYOMING
TETON RANGE
WASATCH RANGE
CONTINENTAL DIVIDE
MOUNTAINS
GREAT
Great Salt Lake
Lake Tahoe
CENTRAL
SIERRA NEVADA
COAST
VALLEY
GREAT BASIN
NEVADA
UTAH
Mt. Elbert 14,433 ft. (4,399 m)
COLORADO
Pikes Peak 14,110 ft. (4,301 m)
PLAINS
NE
North Platte River
South Platte River
San Francisco Bay
Lake Powell
SAN JUAN MTS.
RANGES
Mt. Whitney 14,494 ft. (4,418 m)
DEATH VALLEY
Lake Mead
AZ
Glen Canyon Dam
NM
Rio Grande
Hoover Dam
CALIFORNIA
Colorado River
San Diego Bay
IMPERIAL VALLEY
MEXICO
0   100   200 Miles
0 100 200 300 Kilometers

THE WEST: Elevation

- Dam
- Mountain peak
- ...... Continental divide
- —— Dividing line between Mountain States and Pacific States

Elevations
Feet   Meters
Above 14,000 — Above 4,000
7,000 — 2,000
1,500 — 500
700 — 200
0 — 0
Below sea level

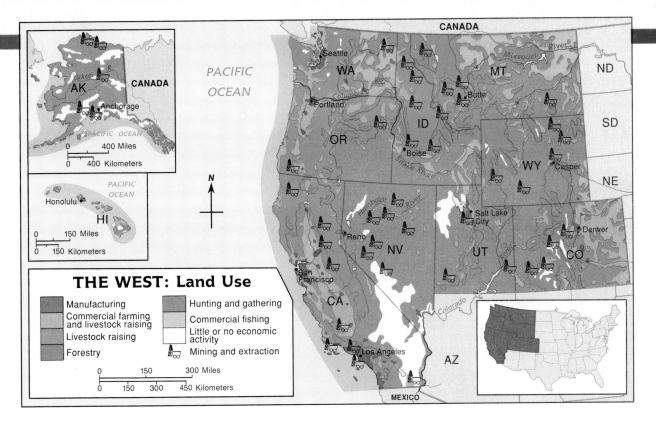

THE WEST: Land Use

- Manufacturing
- Commercial farming and livestock raising
- Livestock raising
- Forestry
- Hunting and gathering
- Commercial fishing
- Little or no economic activity
- Mining and extraction

STATES OF THE WEST

State	Capital	Population	Area in sq mi (sq km)	Date of Statehood
Alaska	Juneau	550,043	656,424 (1,700,138)	1959
California	Sacramento	29,760,021	163,707 (424,001)	1850
Colorado	Denver	3,294,394	104,100 (269,619)	1876
Hawaii	Honolulu	1,108,229	10,392 (28,313)	1959
Idaho	Boise	1,006,749	83,574 (216,457)	1890
Montana	Helena	799,065	147,046 (380,849)	1889
Nevada	Carson City	1,201,833	110,567 (286,369)	1864
Oregon	Salem	2,842,321	98,386 (254,820)	1859
Utah	Salt Lake City	1,722,850	84,904 (219,901)	1896
Washington	Olympia	4,866,692	71,303 (184,675)	1889
Wyoming	Cheyenne	453,588	97,818 (253,349)	1890

Population figures: 1990 Census

LATIN AMERICA

Lifestyles vary greatly in Latin America. Some people live and work in cities. Others live off the land.

Latin America straddles two continents, North America and South America. This vast region stretches from Mexico's border with the United States to the southern tip of South America, and also includes the islands of the Caribbean Sea. Latin America has towering mountains, tropical islands, windswept plains, and the world's largest rain forest. It also houses some of the largest urban areas in the world, including the world's second-largest city—Mexico City.

Latin America gets its name from Latin, an old language that

BRAZIL

Brazil is larger than the 48 states of the continental United States.

This Aztec temple in Mexico and the Incan vase from Peru are part of Latin America's past.

Brazil's Amazon River Basin contains the world's largest rain forest. It is home to wildlife—such as this sloth and frog—found nowhere else in the world.

was the "grandparent" of many languages spoken in Europe. For hundreds of years Latin America was ruled by European countries. Foreign rule greatly affected life in this region. One result is that most of the people in Latin America today speak the "Latin" languages called Spanish and Portuguese.

Two landforms greatly shape life in Latin America—the Andes Mountains and the Amazon River. As you look at the maps in this section, hunt for clues that show how these landforms affect the climate, land use, and settlement of the land around them.

The Andes Mountains in South America are the longest mountain range in the world.

Latin America contains two of the world's largest urban areas, including São Paulo, Brazil (*below*). According to the graph, what is the world's largest urban area?

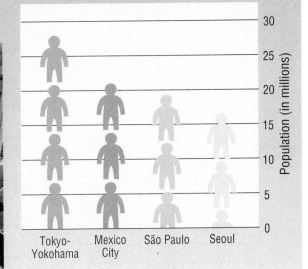

Soccer is the most popular sport in Latin America.

WORLD'S LARGEST URBAN AREAS

Population (in millions)

30
25
20
15
10
5
0

Tokyo-Yokohama   Mexico City   São Paulo   Seoul

34

NORTH

AMERICA

Gulf of California

Baja California

SIERRA MADRE OCCIDENTAL

SIERRA MADRE ORIENTAL

Gulf of Mexico

Yucatán Peninsula

Cuba

Greater Antilles

Hispaniola

Caribbean Sea

Tropic of Cancer

30°N

15°N

CENTRAL

AMERICA

Lake Nicaragua

Isthmus of Panama

Gulf of Panama

Guajira Peninsula

Lake Maracaibo

Lesser Antilles

15°N

LLANOS

Orinoco R.

GUIANA HIGHLANDS

Cauca River

Magdalena River

0° Equator

Galápagos Islands

Gulf of Guayaquil

Aguja Point

ANDES MOUNTAINS

Marañon R.

Japurá

Rio Negro

AMAZON

River

Amazon

River

Marajó Island

0°

Cape São Roque

PACIFIC

BASIN

Tapajós R.

Xingu River

Tocantins River

Parnaíba River

São Francisco River

Ucayali

Purus

Madeira R.

River

SOUTH

MATO GROSSO PLATEAU

OCEAN

15°S

Lake Titicaca

Lake Poopó

AMERICA

Araguaia

BRAZILIAN

15°S

ATACAMA DESERT

ANDES

Pilcomayo

GRAN CHACO

Paraguay R.

River

HIGHLANDS

Tropic of Capricorn

River

Salado

Paraná

River

30°S

MOUNTAINS

Mt. Aconcagua 22,834 ft. (6,960 m)

River

Uruguay

River

ATLANTIC

30°S

PAMPAS

Rio de la Plata

Blanca Bay

Chiloé Island

San Matías Gulf

OCEAN

45°S

PATAGONIA

Gulf of San Jorge

N

45°S

Strait of Magellan

Falkland Islands

Tierra del Fuego

Cape Horn

South Georgia

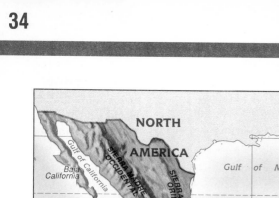

LATIN AMERICA

Physical

0   400   800 Miles

0   400   800   1,200 Kilometers

105°W   90°W   75°W   60°W   45°W

LATIN AMERICA
Political

⊛ National capital   • Other city

0   400   800 Miles

0   400   800   1,200 Kilometers

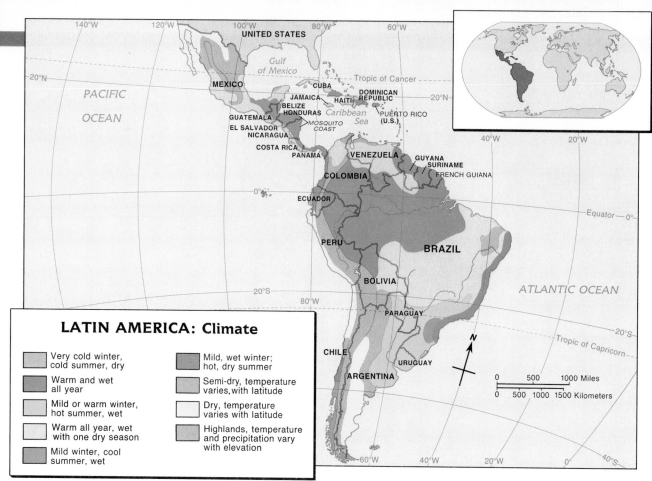

LATIN AMERICA: Climate

- Very cold winter, cold summer, dry
- Warm and wet all year
- Mild or warm winter, hot summer, wet
- Warm all year, wet with one dry season
- Mild winter, cool summer, wet
- Mild, wet winter; hot, dry summer
- Semi-dry, temperature varies with latitude
- Dry, temperature varies with latitude
- Highlands, temperature and precipitation vary with elevation

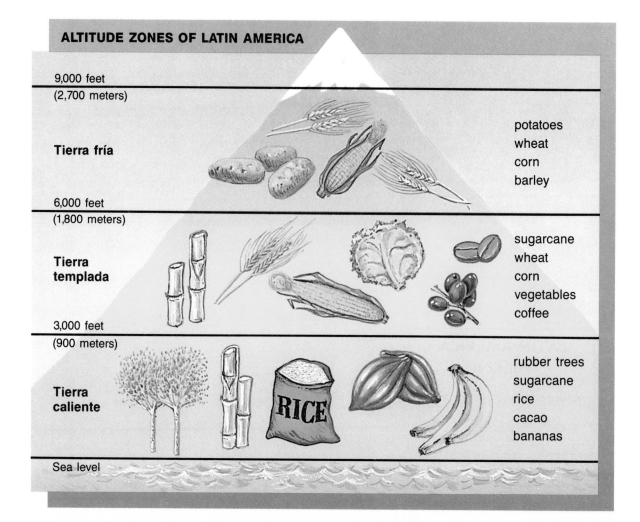

ALTITUDE ZONES OF LATIN AMERICA

9,000 feet
(2,700 meters)

Tierra fría

potatoes
wheat
corn
barley

6,000 feet
(1,800 meters)

Tierra templada

sugarcane
wheat
corn
vegetables
coffee

3,000 feet
(900 meters)

Tierra caliente

RICE

rubber trees
sugarcane
rice
cacao
bananas

Sea level

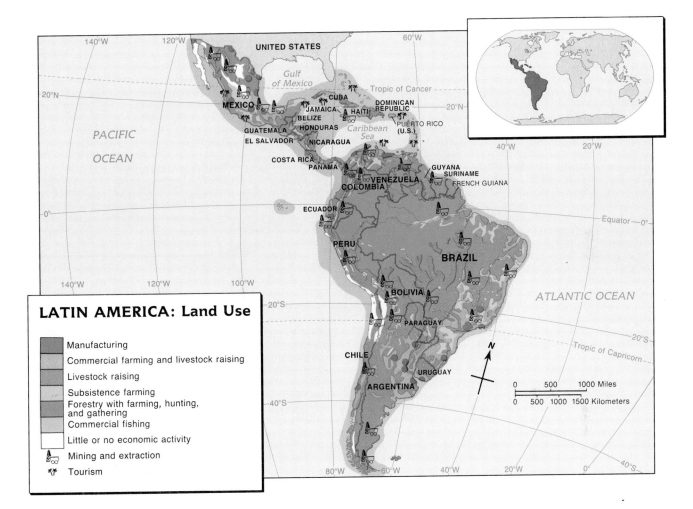

LATIN AMERICA: Land Use

- Manufacturing
- Commercial farming and livestock raising
- Livestock raising
- Subsistence farming
- Forestry with farming, hunting, and gathering
- Commercial fishing
- Little or no economic activity
- Mining and extraction
- Tourism

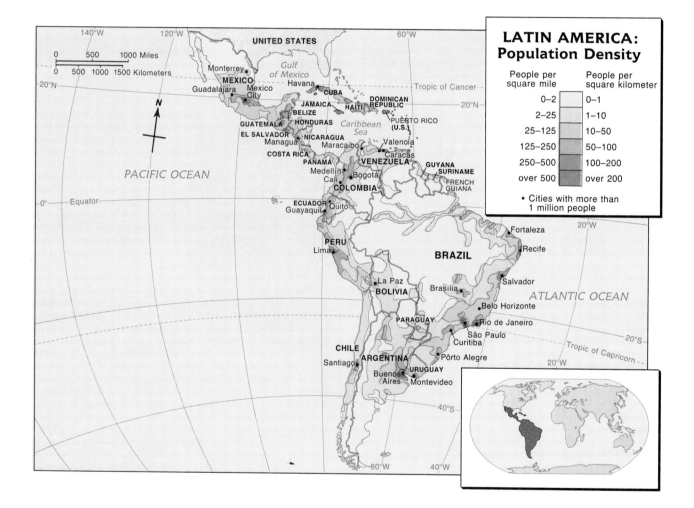

LATIN AMERICA:
Population Density

People per square mile	People per square kilometer
0–2	0–1
2–25	1–10
25–125	10–50
125–250	50–100
250–500	100–200
over 500	over 200

• Cities with more than 1 million people

140°W 120°W 60°W

UNITED STATES

Gulf of Mexico

Monterrey
Guadalajara
MEXICO
Mexico City
Havana
CUBA
Tropic of Cancer
20°N

JAMAICA
BELIZE
HAITI
DOMINICAN REPUBLIC
20°N

GUATEMALA
HONDURAS
EL SALVADOR
NICARAGUA
Managua
COSTA RICA
PANAMA
Maracaibo
Valencia
Caracas
VENEZUELA
PUERTO RICO (U.S.)
Caribbean Sea

Medellín
Cali
Bogotá
COLOMBIA
GUYANA
SURINAME
FRENCH GUIANA

PACIFIC OCEAN

0° Equator

ECUADOR
Guayaquil Quito

Fortaleza
20°W

PERU
Lima

BRAZIL
Recife

La Paz
BOLIVIA
Brasília
Salvador

ATLANTIC OCEAN

Belo Horizonte

PARAGUAY
Rio de Janeiro
São Paulo
Curitiba
20°S
Tropic of Capricorn

CHILE
Pôrto Alegre
20°W

ARGENTINA
Santiago
URUGUAY
Buenos Aires
Montevideo

40°S

60°W 40°W

LATIN AMERICA

Country	Capital	Area in sq mi (sq km)	Population
Antigua/Barbuda	St. John's	170 (440)	100,000
Argentina	Buenos Aires	1,068,299 (2,766,890)	32,700,000
Bahamas	Nassau	5,382 (13,940)	300,000
Barbados	Bridgetown	166 (430)	300,000
Belize	Belmopan	8,865 (22,960)	200,000
Bolivia	La Paz; Sucre	424,163 (1,098,580)	7,500,000
Brazil	Brasilia	3,286,480 (8,511,970)	153,300,000
Chile	Santiago	292,259 (756,950)	13,400,000
Colombia	Bogotá	439,734 (1,138,910)	33,600,000
Costa Rica	San José	19,652 (50,900)	3,100,000
Cuba	Havana	42,803 (110,860)	10,700,000
Dominica	Roseau	290 (750)	100,000
Dominican Republic	Santo Domingo	18,816 (48,730)	7,300,000
Ecuador	Quito	109,483 (283,560)	10,800,000
El Salvador	San Salvador	8,124 (21,040)	5,400,000
French Guiana	Cayenne	35,135 (91,000)	100,000
Grenada	St. George's	131 (340)	100,000
Guatemala	Guatemala City	42,042 (108,890)	9,500,000
Guyana	Georgetown	83,000 (214,970)	800,000
Haiti	Port-au-Prince	10,714 (27,750)	6,300,000
Honduras	Tegucigalpa	43,277 (112,090)	5,300,000
Jamaica	Kingston	4,243 (10,990)	2,500,000
Mexico	Mexico City	761,604 (1,972,550)	85,700,000
Nicaragua	Managua	49,998 (129,494)	3,900,000
Panama	Panama City	30,193 (78,200)	2,500,000
Paraguay	Asunción	157,047 (406,750)	4,400,000
Peru	Lima	496,225 (1,285,200)	22,000,000
Puerto Rico	San Juan	3,515 (9,104)	3,500,000
St. Kitts and Nevis	Basseterre	139 (360)	40,000
St. Lucia	Castries	239 (620)	200,000
St. Vincent/Grenadines	Kingstown	131 (340)	100,000
Suriname	Paramaribo	63,039 (163,270)	400,000
Trinidad/Tobago	Port-of-Spain	1,980 (5,130)	1,300,000
Uruguay	Montevideo	68,039 (175,220)	3,100,000
Venezuela	Caracas	352,143 (912,050)	20,100,000

EUROPE AND NORTHERN ASIA

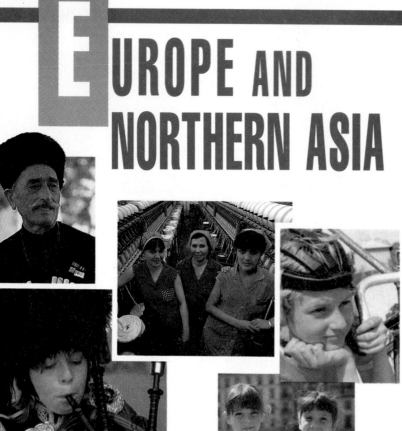

The region of Europe and Northern Asia is home to many different peoples.

Europe and Northern Asia make up the second-largest region in the world. Most of this region was once occupied by the Soviet Union. In 1991 the Soviet Union broke up into 15 independent nations. However, one of these nations—Russia—is still the largest country in the world, spanning two continents and eleven different time zones. While people in western Russia are eating dinner, people in eastern Russia are waking up the next morning!

Europe forms only a very small part of this region. More than

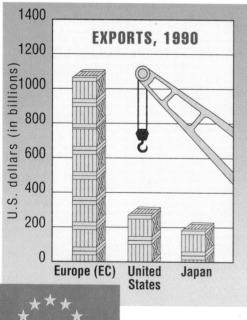

EXPORTS, 1990

U.S. dollars (in billions)

1400
1200
1000
800
600
400
200
0

Europe (EC)   United States   Japan

The Eiffel Tower in Paris, France (*left*) is one of the most famous landmarks of this region.

EC FLAG

Twelve European countries form a special trade partnership called the European Community (EC). As the graph shows, the EC plays a major role in world trade.

forty countries make up an area that is about one half the size of the United States. Despite their sizes, however, these countries have played enormous roles throughout world history.

The location of Europe and Northern Asia has helped this region to play an important part in world affairs. As you look at the maps on the following pages, take special note of how the continents of Europe and Asia come together in this region. Then make some conclusions about how this link between two continents may have helped the region to grow in power and influence throughout history.

Russia is nearly twice the size of the entire United States in land area.

A 32-mile (51-km) railroad tunnel is being built under the English Channel. When the "chunnel" is completed, it will provide the first train link between England and the rest of Europe.

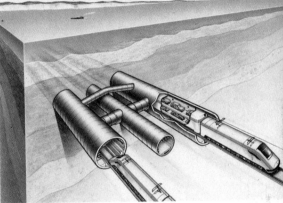

© 1990 The New York Times. Illustration by Hank Iken

St. Basil's Cathedral *(right)* is located in the heart of Moscow, the capital of Russia.

The Caucasus Mountains form part of the southern border of Russia.

Every year thousands of people come to see St. Peter's Square in Vatican City (*left*).

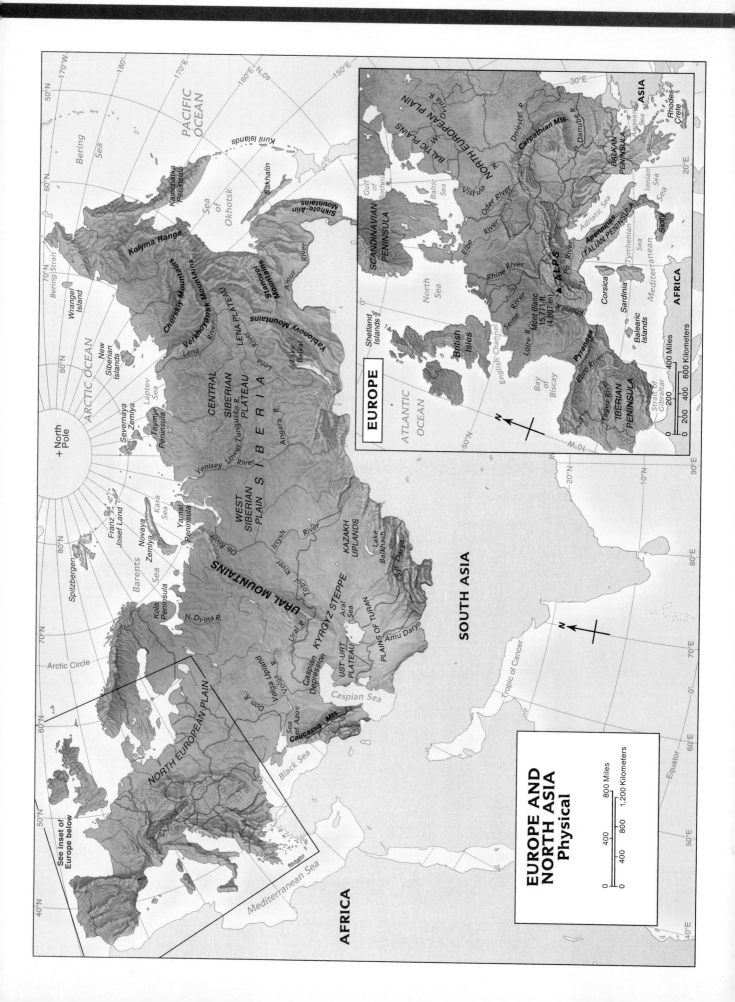

PACIFIC OCEAN

Bering Sea

Kuril Islands

Kamchatka Peninsula

Sea of Okhotsk

Sakhalin

Sikhote-Alin Mountains

Kolyma Range

Chersky Mountains

Verkhoyansk Mountains

Stanovoi Mountains

Yablonovy Mountains

Amur River

Lena PLATEAU

Lena River

Lake Baikal

Bering Strait

ARCTIC OCEAN

Wrangel Island

New Siberian Islands

Laptev Sea

Taymyr Peninsula

Severnaya Zemlya

CENTRAL SIBERIAN PLATEAU

Lower Tunguska R.

S I B E R I A

+ North Pole

Yenisey River

Angara R.

Franz Josef Land

Novaya Zemlya

Kara Sea

WEST SIBERIAN PLAIN

Yamal Peninsula

Ob River

Irtysh River

Spitzbergen

Barents Sea

Kola Peninsula

N. Dvina R.

URAL MOUNTAINS

Tobol River

Arctic Circle

Volga Upland

Volga R.

Don R.

Ural R.

KYRGYZ STEPPE

Caspian Depression

UST'-URT PLATEAU

PLAINS OF TURAN

Amu Darya

Aral Sea

Syr Darya

Lake Balkhash

KAZAKH UPLANDS

SOUTH ASIA

Caspian Sea

Sea of Azov

Caucasus Mts.

Black Sea

NORTH EUROPEAN PLAIN

See inset of Europe below

Mediterranean Sea

AFRICA

Tropic of Cancer

Equator

170°W 180° 170°E 160°E 150°E
50°N 60°N 70°N 80°N 70°N 60°N 50°N 40°N
90°E 80°E 70°E 60°E 50°E 40°E
10°N 20°N

EUROPE AND NORTH ASIA Physical

800 Miles
400
0
1,200 Kilometers
800
400
0

N

Inset — EUROPE

NORTH EUROPEAN PLAIN

SCANDINAVIAN PENINSULA

Gulf of Bothnia

BALTIC PLAINS

Baltic Sea

Vistula R.

Oder River

Elbe River

Rhine River

Seine River

Loire R.

W. Dvina R.

Dniester R.

Carpathian Mts.

Danube R.

Po River

ALPS

Mont Blanc 15,771 ft (4,807 m)

Rhône R.

Apennines

ITALIAN PENINSULA

Pyrenees

Ebro River

Tagus River

IBERIAN PENINSULA

Strait of Gibraltar

BALKAN PENINSULA

Aegean Sea

Rhodes

Crete

Adriatic Sea

Ionian Sea

Tyrrhenian Sea

Corsica

Sardinia

Sicily

Balearic Islands

Mediterranean Sea

Shetland Islands

North Sea

British Isles

English Channel

Bay of Biscay

ATLANTIC OCEAN

ASIA

AFRICA

EUROPE

10°W 0° 20°E 30°E
50°N

N

400 Miles
200
0
600 Kilometers
400
200
0

AFRICA

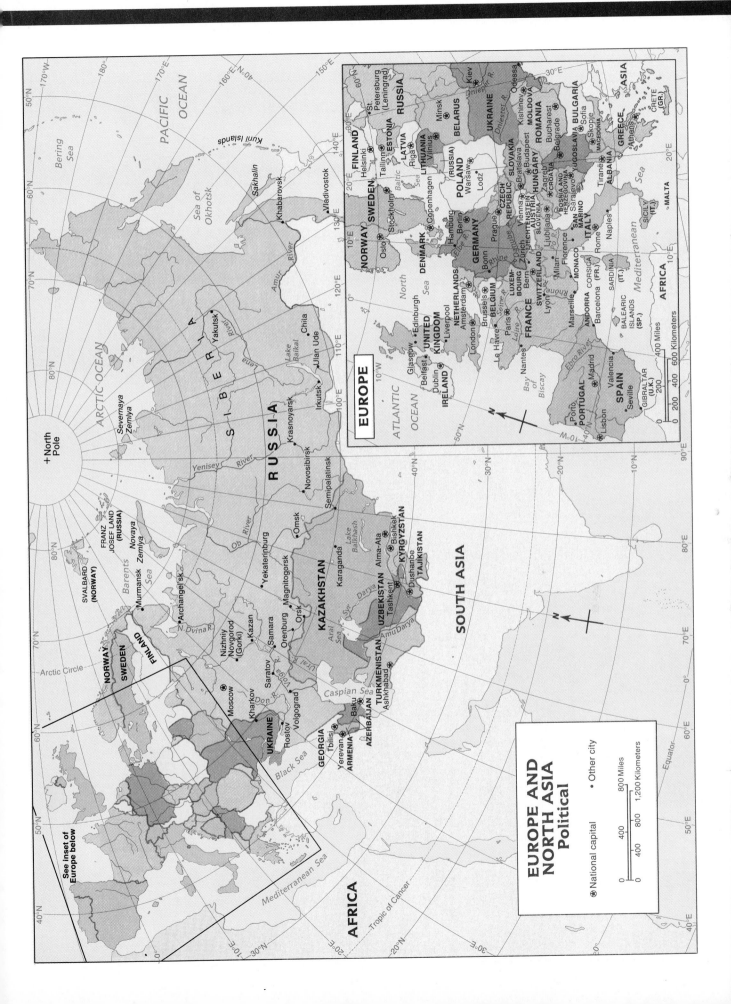

PACIFIC OCEAN

Bering Sea

Kuril Islands

Sea of Okhotsk

Sakhalin

Khabarovsk

Vladivostok

ARCTIC OCEAN

North Pole

Severnaya Zemlya

S I B E R I A

Yakutsk

Lena River

Chita

Ulan Ude

Lake Baikal

Irkutsk

Amur River

RUSSIA

Krasnoyarsk

Novosibirsk

Semipalatinsk

Omsk

Yenisey River

Ob River

FRANZ JOSEF LAND (RUSSIA)

Novaya Zemlya

SVALBARD (NORWAY)

Barents Sea

Murmansk

Archangel'sk

N. Dvina R.

KAZAKHSTAN

Karaganda

Lake Balkhash

Alma-Ata

Bishkek

KYRGYZSTAN

Dushanbe

TAJIKISTAN

Yekaterinburg

Magnitogorsk

Orenburg

Orsk

Syr Darya

Aral Sea

UZBEKISTAN

Tashkent

TURKMENISTAN

Ashkhabad

Amu Darya

Ural R.

Nizhniy Novgorod (Gorki)

Kazan

Samara

Saratov

Volga R.

Moscow

Kharkov

UKRAINE

Rostov

Volgograd

Don R.

Caspian Sea

Baku

AZERBAIJAN

GEORGIA

Tbilisi

ARMENIA

Yerevan

Black Sea

Arctic Circle

NORWAY

SWEDEN

FINLAND

SOUTH ASIA

AFRICA

Mediterranean Sea

Tropic of Cancer

Equator

See inset of Europe below

EUROPE AND NORTH ASIA
Political

⊛ National capital   • Other city

0   400   800 Miles
0   400   800   1,200 Kilometers

EUROPE

RUSSIA

St. Petersburg (Leningrad)

Kiev

Odessa

UKRAINE

Dnieper R.

Minsk

BELARUS

Kishinev

MOLDOVA

ROMANIA

Bucharest

BULGARIA

Sofia

Belgrade

YUGOSLAVIA

Skopje

MACEDONIA

GREECE

Athens

ASIA

CRETE (GR.)

FINLAND

Helsinki

ESTONIA

Tallinn

LATVIA

Riga

LITHUANIA

Vilnius

(RUSSIA)

POLAND

Warsaw

Lodz

SLOVAKIA

Bratislava

HUNGARY

Budapest

CROATIA

Zagreb

BOSNIA AND HERZEGOVINA

Sarajevo

San Marino

SAN MARINO

Tiranë

ALBANIA

MALTA

SICILY (IT.)

Naples

NORWAY

SWEDEN

Oslo

Stockholm

Baltic Sea

DENMARK

Copenhagen

North Sea

Hamburg

Berlin

GERMANY

Bonn

Prague

CZECH REPUBLIC

Vienna

AUSTRIA

LIECHTENSTEIN

Ljubljana

SLOVENIA

Danube R.

Zürich

SWITZERLAND

Bern

MONACO

Milan

Florence

ITALY

Rome

Mediterranean Sea

AFRICA

Elbe R.

Rhine R.

NETHERLANDS

Amsterdam

BELGIUM

Brussels

LUXEMBOURG

Paris

FRANCE

Le Havre

Seine

Loire

Lyon

Rhône

Marseille

ANDORRA

CORSICA (FR.)

SARDINIA (IT.)

UNITED KINGDOM

Edinburgh

Glasgow

Belfast

Dublin

IRELAND

Liverpool

London

ATLANTIC OCEAN

Bay of Biscay

Nantes

Barcelona

BALEARIC ISLANDS (SP.)

Ebro River

Madrid

Valencia

SPAIN

Seville

PORTUGAL

Porto

Lisbon

GIBRALTAR (U.K.)

EUROPE

N

0   200   400 Miles
0   200   400   600 Kilometers

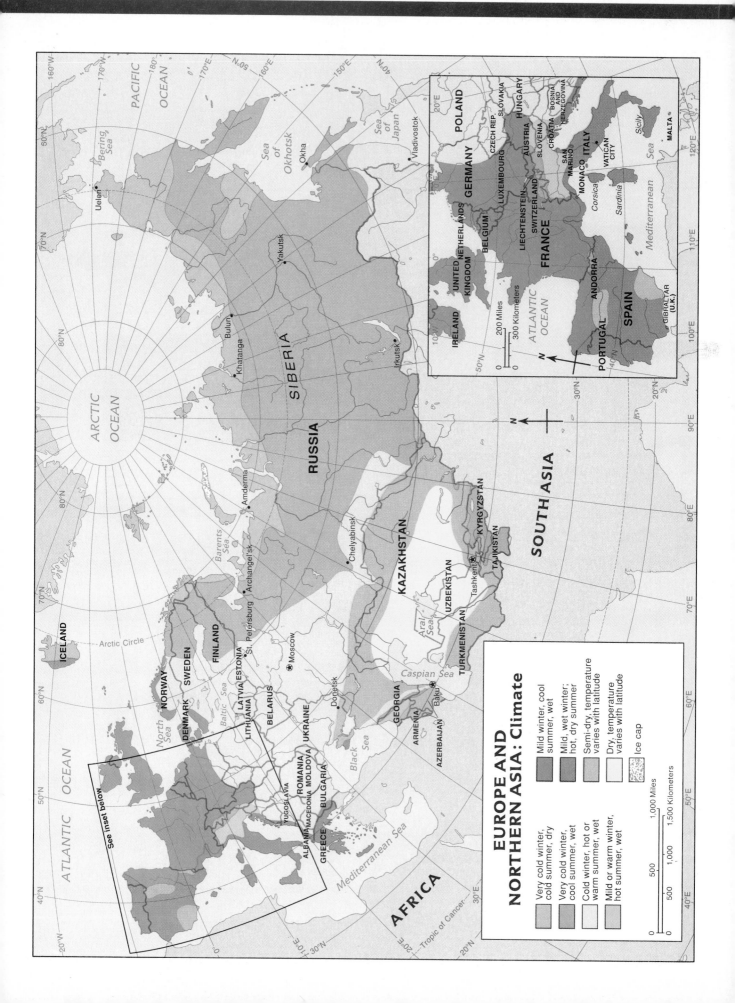

EUROPE AND NORTHERN ASIA: Climate

Very cold winter, cold summer, dry

Very cold winter, cool summer, wet

Cold winter, hot or warm summer, wet

Mild or warm winter, hot summer, wet

Mild winter, cool summer, wet

Mild, wet winter; hot, dry summer

Semi-dry, temperature varies with latitude

Dry, temperature varies with latitude

Ice cap

0   500   1,000
0   500   1,000   1,500 Kilometers

0   200   300 Kilometers
0   300 Miles

See inset below

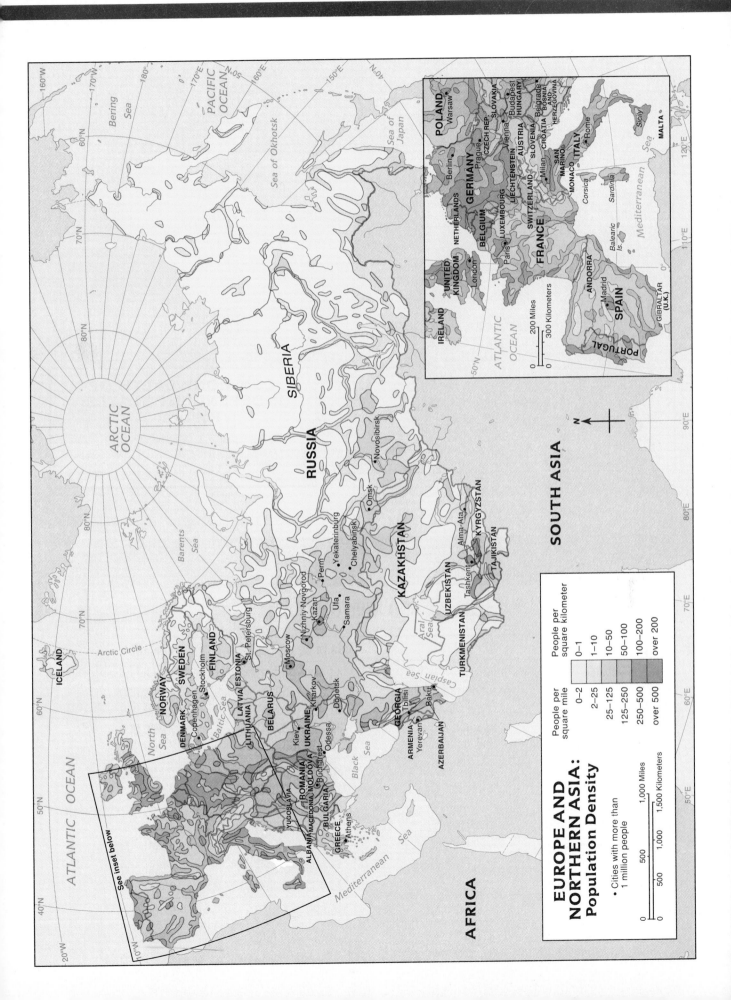

EUROPE AND NORTHERN ASIA: Population Density

• Cities with more than 1 million people

People per square mile / **People per square kilometer**

People per square mile	People per square kilometer
0–2	0–1
2–25	1–10
25–125	10–50
125–250	50–100
250–500	100–200
over 500	over 200

Scale: 0 — 500 — 1,000 Miles
0 — 500 — 1,000 — 1,500 Kilometers

ARCTIC OCEAN

ATLANTIC OCEAN

PACIFIC OCEAN

Bering Sea

Sea of Okhotsk

Sea of Japan

SIBERIA

RUSSIA

KAZAKHSTAN

SOUTH ASIA

AFRICA

ICELAND
NORWAY
SWEDEN
FINLAND
DENMARK
Copenhagen
Stockholm
St. Petersburg
Moscow
ESTONIA
LATVIA
LITHUANIA
BELARUS
UKRAINE
Kiev
Kharkov
Odessa
Donetsk
MOLDOVA
ROMANIA
Bucharest
YUGOSLAVIA
ALBANIA
MACEDONIA
BULGARIA
GREECE
Athens
GEORGIA
Tbilisi
ARMENIA
Yerevan
AZERBAIJAN
Baku
Nizhniy Novgorod
Kazan
Samara
Perm
Ufa
Yekaterinburg
Chelyabinsk
Omsk
Novosibirsk
UZBEKISTAN
Tashkent
TURKMENISTAN
TAJIKISTAN
KYRGYZSTAN
Alma-Ata
Aral Sea
Caspian Sea
Black Sea
Baltic Sea
North Sea
Barents Sea
Mediterranean Sea
Arctic Circle

See inset below

Inset:

ATLANTIC OCEAN
Mediterranean Sea

IRELAND
UNITED KINGDOM
London
NETHERLANDS
BELGIUM
LUXEMBOURG
FRANCE
Paris
GERMANY
Berlin
POLAND
Warsaw
CZECH REP.
Prague
SLOVAKIA
AUSTRIA
Vienna
HUNGARY
Budapest
SLOVENIA
CROATIA
BOSNIA AND HERZEGOVINA
SERBIA
Belgrade
SWITZERLAND
LIECHTENSTEIN
Milan
ITALY
Rome
SAN MARINO
MONACO
Corsica
Sardinia
Sicily
MALTA
SPAIN
Madrid
ANDORRA
PORTUGAL
GIBRALTAR (U.K.)
Balearic Is.

200 Miles
300 Kilometers

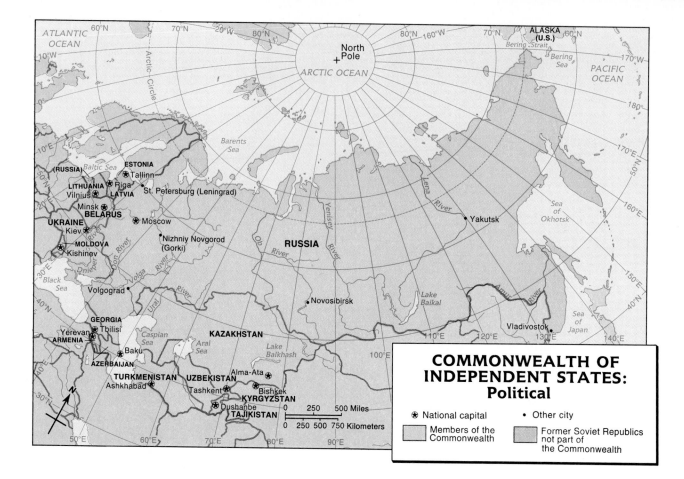

EUROPE AND NORTHERN ASIA

Country	Capital	Area in sq mi (sq km)	Population
Albania	Tiranë	11,100 (28,750)	3,300,000
Andorra	Andorra la Vella	174 (450)	53,000
Armenia	Yerevan	11,490 (29,800)	3,300,000
Austria	Vienna	32,375 (83,850)	7,700,000
Azerbaijan	Baku	33,430 (86,600)	7,100,000
Belarus	Minsk	80,134 (207,600)	10,300,000
Belgium	Brussels	11,779 (30,510)	9,900,000
Bosnia and Herzegovina	Sarajevo	19,741 (51,129)	4,100,000
Bulgaria	Sofia	42,822 (110,910)	9,000,000
Croatia	Zagreb	21,829 (56,537)	4,600,000
Czech Repubic	Prague	30,400 (78,864)	10,400,000
Denmark	Copenhagen	16,629 (43,070)	5,100,000
Estonia	Tallinn	17,413 (45,100)	1,600,000

Finland	Helsinki	130,128 (337,030)	5,000,000
France	Paris	211,209 (547,030)	56,700,000
Georgia	Tbilisi	26,900 (69,700)	5,500,000
Germany	Berlin	137,803 (356,910)	79,500,000
Greece	Athens	50,942 (131,940)	10,100,000
Hungary	Budapest	35,919 (93,030)	10,400,000
Iceland	Reykjavik	39,768 (103,000)	300,000
Ireland	Dublin	27,135 (70,820)	3,500,000
Italy	Rome	116,305 (301,230)	57,700,000
Kazakhstan	Alma-Ata	1,049,155 (2,717,300)	16,700,000
Kyrgyzstan	Bishkek	76,640 (198,500)	4,400,000
Latvia	Riga	24,595 (63,700)	2,700,000
Liechtenstein	Vaduz	62 (160)	30,000
Lithuania	Vilnius	25,170 (65,200)	3,700,000
Luxembourg	Luxembourg	988 (2,586)	400,000
Macedonia	Skopje	9,928 (25,713)	1,900,000
Malta	Valletta	123 (320)	400,000
Moldova	Kishinev	13,000 (33,700)	4,400,000
Monaco	Monaco	0.7 (1.9)	30,000
Netherlands, The	Amsterdam	14,405 (37,310)	15,000,000
Norway	Oslo	125,182 (324,220)	4,300,000
Poland	Warsaw	120,726 (312,680)	38,200,000
Portugal	Lisbon	35,552 (92,080)	10,400,000
Romania	Bucharest	91,699 (237,500)	23,400,000
Russia	Moscow	6,592,813 (17,075,000)	148,000,000
San Marino	San Marino	23 (60)	23,000
Slovakia	Bratislava	18,932 (49,035)	5,300,000
Slovenia	Ljubljana	7,819 (20,251)	1,900,000
Spain	Madrid	194,884 (504,750)	39,000,000
Sweden	Stockholm	173,730 (449,960)	8,600,000
Switzerland	Bern	15,942 (41,290)	6,800,000
Tajikistan	Dushanbe	55,240 (143,100)	5,300,000
Turkmenistan	Ashkhabad	186,400 (488,100)	3,600,000
Ukraine	Kiev	231,990 (445,000)	51,800,000
United Kingdom	London	94,525 (244,820)	57,500,000
Uzbekistan	Tashkent	172,741 (447,400)	20,300,000
Vatican City	Vatican City	0.17 (0.44)	750
Yugoslavia	Belgrade	39,449 (102,173)	10,200,000

MIDDLE EAST AND NORTH AFRICA

This Israeli farm boy, Arab student, and North African shepherd girl represent three of the groups that live in the Middle East and North Africa.

The Middle East and North Africa form a meeting ground between three continents—Africa, Asia, and Europe. Throughout history this region has been an important crossroads for goods and ideas from these three continents. African, Asian, and European civilizations grew and learned from each other because of the traders who crossed the seas, deserts, and mountains of this region.

Along with fertile river valleys and plains, this region includes some of the hottest, driest places on earth. It gets so hot, in fact,

Israel is a leading exporter of citrus fruits. There, crops are grown on land reclaimed from the desert.

SAUDI ARABIA

Saudi Arabia is about one third the size of the 48 states of the continental United States.

that thermometers have burst in the midday sun! Not surprisingly, water is a precious natural resource throughout the region.

Another important natural resource is oil. Oil has brought great wealth to parts of this region. But it has also caused much conflict as people struggle for control over this valuable resource.

As you look at the maps of this region, identify the countries that have benefited the most from oil production in the Middle East and North Africa. Also try to determine how the need for water has shaped settlement in this region.

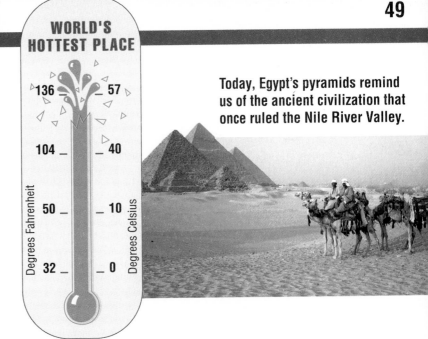

WORLD'S HOTTEST PLACE

Degrees Fahrenheit | Degrees Celsius
136 — — 57
104 — — 40
50 — — 10
32 — — 0

The hottest place on earth is Al'Aziziyah, Libya. In 1922 a temperature of 136°F. (57°C) was recorded there.

Today, Egypt's pyramids remind us of the ancient civilization that once ruled the Nile River Valley.

Jerusalem is an important city for people of three different religious faiths.

The Aswan Dam, on the Nile River in Egypt, provides a steady water supply for many farmers.

US/Canada 4%
South & East Asia 5%
Sub-Saharan Africa 6%
Europe/Northern Asia 8%
Latin America 13%
Middle East and North Africa 64%

WORLD OIL RESERVES

Oil has made the Middle East and North Africa one of the wealthiest regions in the world. Use the chart to learn the percentage of the world's oil reserves found in this region.

Egypt's Suez Canal, 105 miles (168 km) long, is one of the world's most important human-made waterways. It first opened in 1869.

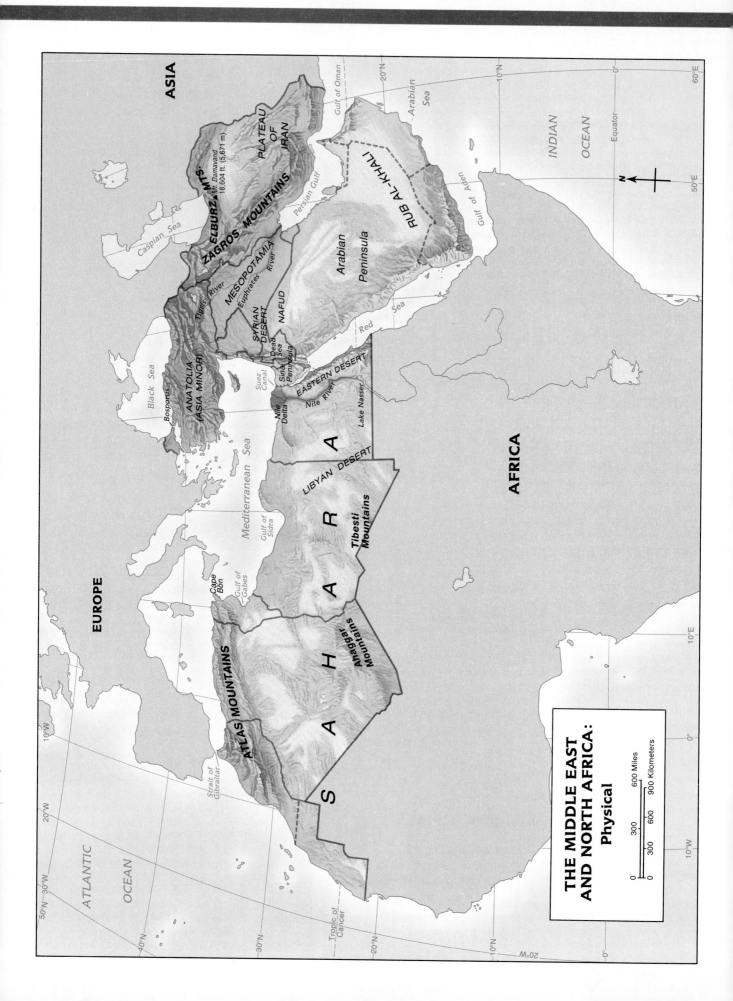

ASIA

PLATEAU OF IRAN

ELBURZ MTS
Mt. Damavand
18,604 ft. (5,671 m)

ZAGROS MOUNTAINS

Gulf of Oman

Arabian Sea

INDIAN OCEAN

Equator

Caspian Sea

MESOPOTAMIA

Tigris River

Euphrates River

Persian Gulf

RUB AL-KHALI

Arabian Peninsula

SYRIAN DESERT

NAFUD

Dead Sea

Black Sea

ANATOLIA (ASIA MINOR)

Bosporus

Suez Canal

Sinai Peninsula

EASTERN DESERT

Nile Delta

Nile River

Lake Nasser

Red Sea

Gulf of Aden

AFRICA

Mediterranean Sea

Gulf of Sidra

EUROPE

LIBYAN DESERT

S A H A R A

Tibesti Mountains

Cape Bon

Gulf of Gabes

ATLAS MOUNTAINS

Ahaggar Mountains

Strait of Gibraltar

ATLANTIC OCEAN

Tropic of Cancer

THE MIDDLE EAST
AND NORTH AFRICA:
Physical

600 Miles
300
900 Kilometers
600
300
0
0

60°E
50°E
20°N
10°N
10°E
0°
10°W
20°W
30°W
40°N
50°N
30°N
20°N
10°N
20°W

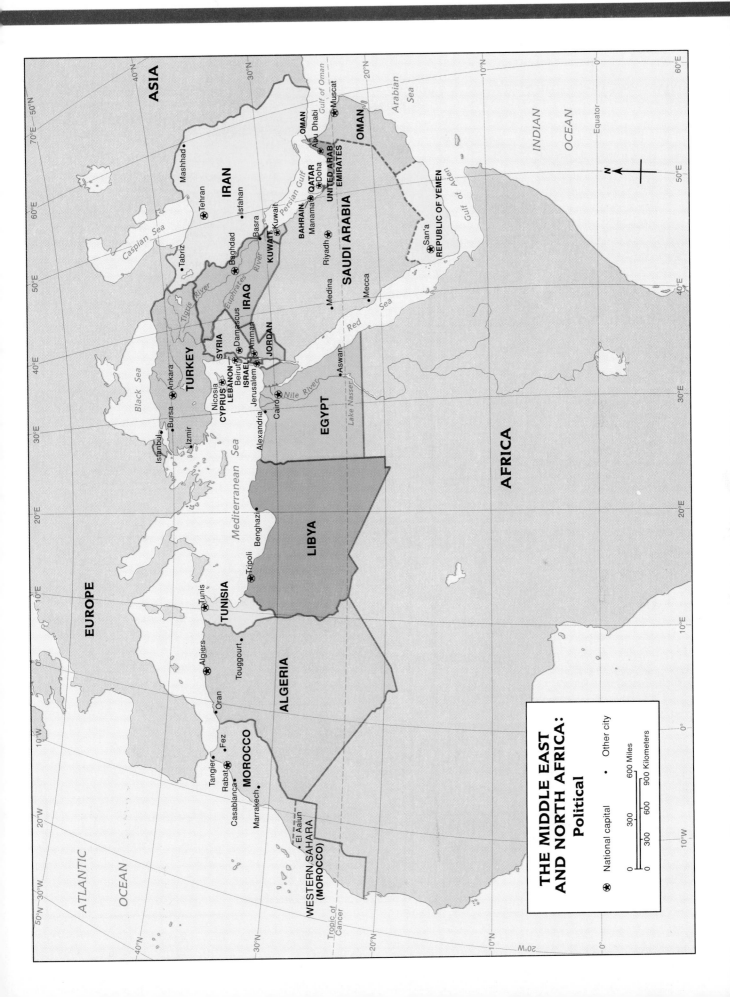

ASIA

EUROPE

ATLANTIC OCEAN

INDIAN OCEAN

AFRICA

Caspian Sea

Black Sea

Mediterranean Sea

Red Sea

Persian Gulf

Gulf of Oman

Arabian Sea

Gulf of Aden

Equator

Tropic of Cancer

IRAN
- Mashhad
- Tehran
- Isfahan
- Tabriz

TURKEY
- Ankara
- Bursa
- Istanbul
- Izmir

IRAQ
- Baghdad
- Basra

Tigris River
Euphrates River
Nile River
Lake Nasser

SYRIA
- Damascus

LEBANON
- Beirut

CYPRUS
- Nicosia

ISRAEL
- Jerusalem

JORDAN
- Amman

KUWAIT
- Kuwait

OMAN
- Muscat
- Abu Dhabi

QATAR
- Doha

BAHRAIN
- Manama

UNITED ARAB EMIRATES

SAUDI ARABIA
- Riyadh
- Medina
- Mecca

REPUBLIC OF YEMEN
- San'a

EGYPT
- Cairo
- Alexandria
- Aswan

LIBYA
- Tripoli
- Benghazi

TUNISIA
- Tunis

ALGERIA
- Algiers
- Oran
- Touggourt

MOROCCO
- Rabat
- Tangier
- Casablanca
- Fez
- Marrakech

WESTERN SAHARA (MOROCCO)
- El Aaiun

THE MIDDLE EAST AND NORTH AFRICA:
Political

⊛ National capital   • Other city

| 600 Miles |
| 300 |
| 900 Kilometers |
| 300 | 600 |

50°N · 40°N · 30°N · 20°N · 10°N
70°E · 60°E · 50°E · 40°E · 30°E · 20°E · 10°E · 0° · 10°W · 20°W · 30°W
60°E · 50°E · 40°E · 30°E · 20°E · 10°E · 0° · 10°W · 20°W

52

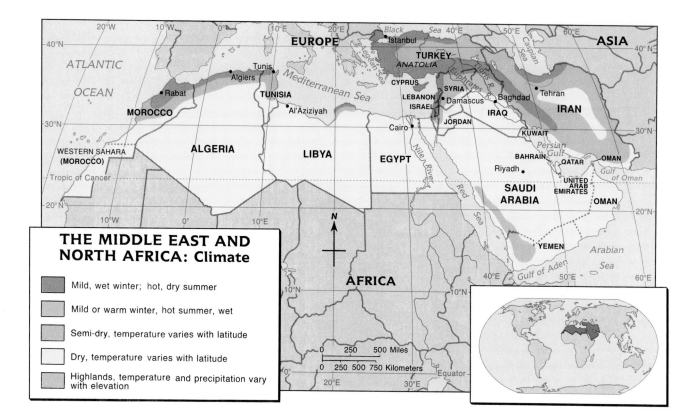

THE MIDDLE EAST AND NORTH AFRICA: Climate

- Mild, wet winter; hot, dry summer
- Mild or warm winter, hot summer, wet
- Semi-dry, temperature varies with latitude
- Dry, temperature varies with latitude
- Highlands, temperature and precipitation vary with elevation

0 250 500 Miles
0 250 500 750 Kilometers

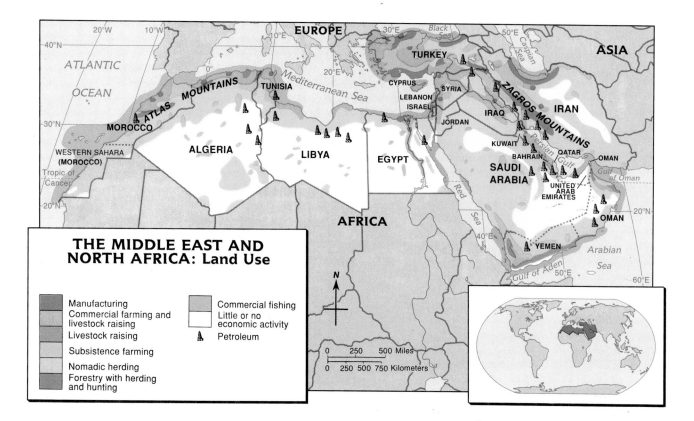

THE MIDDLE EAST AND NORTH AFRICA: Land Use

- Manufacturing
- Commercial farming and livestock raising
- Livestock raising
- Subsistence farming
- Nomadic herding
- Forestry with herding and hunting
- Commercial fishing
- Little or no economic activity
- Petroleum

0 250 500 Miles
0 250 500 750 Kilometers

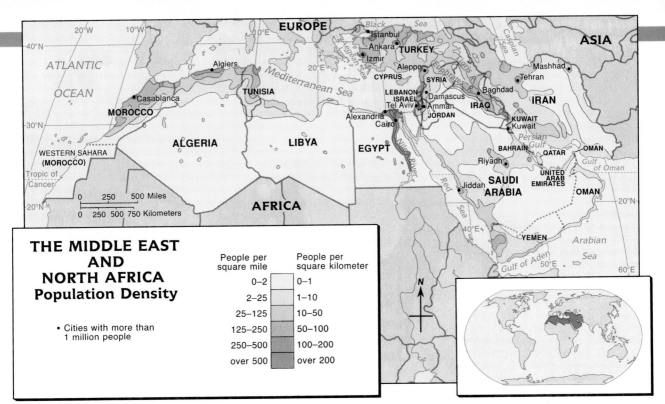

THE MIDDLE EAST
AND
NORTH AFRICA
Population Density

People per square mile		People per square kilometer
0–2		0–1
2–25		1–10
25–125		10–50
125–250		50–100
250–500		100–200
over 500		over 200

• Cities with more than 1 million people

THE MIDDLE EAST AND NORTH AFRICA

Country	Capital	Area in sq mi (sq km)	Population
Algeria	Algiers	919,592 (2,381,740)	26,000,000
Bahrain	Manama	239 (620)	500,000
Cyprus	Nicosia	3,571 (9,250)	700,000
Egypt	Cairo	386,661 (1,001,450)	54,500,000
Iran	Tehran	636,294 (1,648,000)	58,600,000
Iraq	Baghdad	167,923 (434,920)	17,100,000
Israel	Jerusalem	8,091 (20,770)	4,900,000
Jordan	Amman	35,475 (91,880)	3,400,000
Kuwait	Kuwait	6,880 (17,820)	1,400,000
Lebanon	Beirut	4,015 (10,400)	3,400,000
Libya	Tripoli	679,360 (1,759,540)	4,400,000
Morocco	Rabat	172,413 (446,550)	26,200,000
Oman	Muscat	82,013 (212,460)	1,600,000
Qatar	Doha	4,247 (11,000)	500,000
Saudi Arabia	Riyadh	829,997 (2,149,690)	15,500,000
Syria	Damascus	71,498 (185,180)	12,800,000
Tunisia	Tunis	63,170 (163,610)	8,400,000
Turkey	Ankara	301,383 (780,580)	58,500,000
United Arab Emirates	Abu Dhabi	32,278 (83,600)	2,400,000
Yemen	San'a	203,850 (527,970)	10,100,000

SUB-SAHARAN AFRICA

As in all regions, children are the future of Sub-Saharan Africa. Almost half of the people of this region are under the age of 15.

The continent of Africa is split into two regions by the Sahara, the world's largest desert. North Africa is a hot and dry region that shares cultural ties with the Middle East. By contrast, Africa below the Sahara—or "Sub-Saharan" Africa—has many different landforms and ways of life.

Sub-Saharan Africa is a vast region that contains more land than all of North America. In some places you will find hot

SAHARA

Lions, zebras, and other wildlife live on the plains below Mount Kilimanjaro, Africa's tallest mountain.

The Sahara is larger than the 48 states of the continental United States. The desert continues to grow each year, destroying farmland and causing millions of people to go hungry.

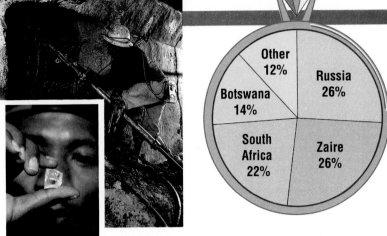

and dry landforms like those in North Africa. Elsewhere you will find rain forests, ice-capped mountains, dramatic waterfalls, and large lakes.

For some people Sub-Saharan Africa is a lush storehouse of beauty and natural resources. For many others this land they call home demands an endless struggle to survive each new day. As you look at the maps of this region, look for the many different landforms that are located in Sub-Saharan Africa.

Most of the world's diamonds come from countries in Sub-Saharan Africa, as the graph shows. People work in tunnels dug deep into the earth to recover gems like the one shown above.

Sub-Saharan Africa is a region of both busy cities and small villages, such as these in West Africa.

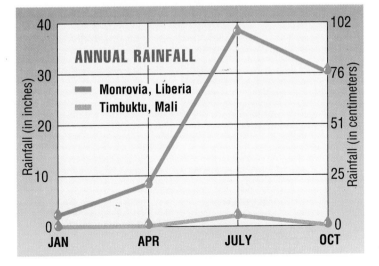

Annual rainfall varies greatly in Sub-Saharan Africa. According to the graph, how much rain falls in Monrovia, Liberia, and Timbuktu, Mali, in July?

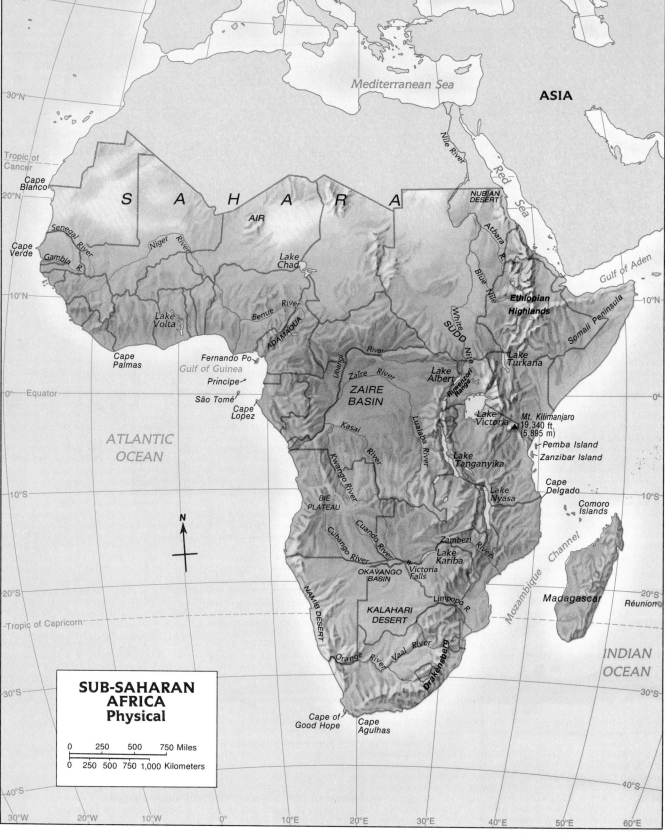

EUROPE

ATLANTIC OCEAN

Mediterranean Sea

ASIA

Tropic of Cancer

Cape Blanco

S A H A R A

AIR

NUBIAN DESERT

Nile River

Red Sea

Cape Verde

Senegal River

Gambia R.

Niger River

Lake Chad

Atbara R.

Gulf of Aden

Benue River

Blue Nile

White Nile

Ethiopian Highlands

SUDD

Somali Peninsula

Lake Volta

ADAMAOUA

Cape Palmas

Fernando Po

Gulf of Guinea

Príncipe

São Tomé

Cape Lopez

Ubangi

Zaïre River

River

ZAIRE BASIN

Lake Albert

Lake Turkana

Ruwenzori Range

Equator

ATLANTIC OCEAN

Kasai

Lualaba River

Lake Victoria

Mt. Kilimanjaro 19,340 ft. (5,895 m)

Kwango River

River

Lake Tanganyika

Pemba Island

Zanzibar Island

Cape Delgado

BIE PLATEAU

Lake Nyasa

Comoro Islands

N

Cuando River

Zambezi River

Cubango River

Lake Kariba

Victoria Falls

Mozambique Channel

NAMIB DESERT

OKAVANGO BASIN

Limpopo R.

Madagascar

Réunion

Tropic of Capricorn

KALAHARI DESERT

Orange River

Vaal River

Drakensberg

INDIAN OCEAN

SUB-SAHARAN AFRICA Physical

0 250 500 750 Miles
0 250 500 750 1,000 Kilometers

Cape of Good Hope

Cape Agulhas

ATLANTIC OCEAN

EUROPE

Mediterranean Sea

ASIA

Nile River

Red Sea

Tropic of Cancer

Gulf of Aden

MAURITANIA

Nouakchott ⊛

MALI
• Timbuktu

NIGER

CHAD

Port Sudan •

ERITREA
★ Asmara

SENEGAL
Dakar ⊛
Banjul ⊛

GAMBIA

Bamako ⊛

Senegal River

Niger River

Niamey ⊛

Khartoum ⊛

SUDAN

DJIBOUTI
Djibouti •

Bissau ⊕

GUINEA-BISSAU

BURKINA FASO

Ouagadougou ⊛

• Kano

N'Djamena •

Lake Chad

ETHIOPIA
⊛ Addis Ababa

Conakry ⊛

GUINEA

BENIN

GHANA

NIGERIA

Abuja ⊛

Benue River

CENTRAL AFRICAN REPUBLIC

SOMALIA

Freetown ⊛

SIERRA LEONE

CÔTE D'IVOIRE

Lake Volta

TOGO

Porto-Novo ⊛

Lagos •

Lomé •

Accra ⊛

Monrovia ⊛

LIBERIA

Yamoussoukro ⊛

CAMEROON

• Yaoundé

Bangui •

UGANDA

Kampala ⊛

KENYA

Mogadishu •

Malabo ⊛

EQUATORIAL GUINEA

SÃO TOMÉ AND PRÍNCIPE

São Tomé •

Libreville ⊛

CONGO

GABON

Zaïre River

ZAIRE

Kisangani •

Kigali ⊛

RWANDA

Bujumbura ⊛

BURUNDI

Lake Victoria

Nairobi ⊛

Mombasa •

Pemba

Zanzibar

Victoria ⊛

Brazzaville ⊛

Kinshasa ⊛

Kananga •

TANZANIA

Dar es Salaam •

SEYCHELLES

CABINDA (ANGOLA)

Luanda ⊛

ATLANTIC OCEAN

Equator

ANGOLA

ZAMBIA

Lusaka ⊛

Lilongwe ⊛

Zambezi River

Moroni ⊛

COMOROS

MAYOTTE (FR.)

MALAWI

Harare ⊛

ZIMBABWE

MOZAMBIQUE

Antananarivo ⊛

MADAGASCAR

NAMIBIA

Windhoek ⊛

BOTSWANA

Gaborone ⊛

Pretoria ⊛

Johannesburg •

Maputo ⊛

Mbabane ⊛

SWAZILAND

RÉUNION (FR.)

INDIAN OCEAN

Orange River

Bloemfontein ⊛

Maseru ⊛

Durban •

SOUTH AFRICA

LESOTHO

Tropic of Capricorn

Cape Town ⊛

• Port Elizabeth

N
↑

SUB-SAHARAN AFRICA Political

⊛ National capital   • Other city

0   250   500   750 Miles

0   250 500 750 1,000 Kilometers

58

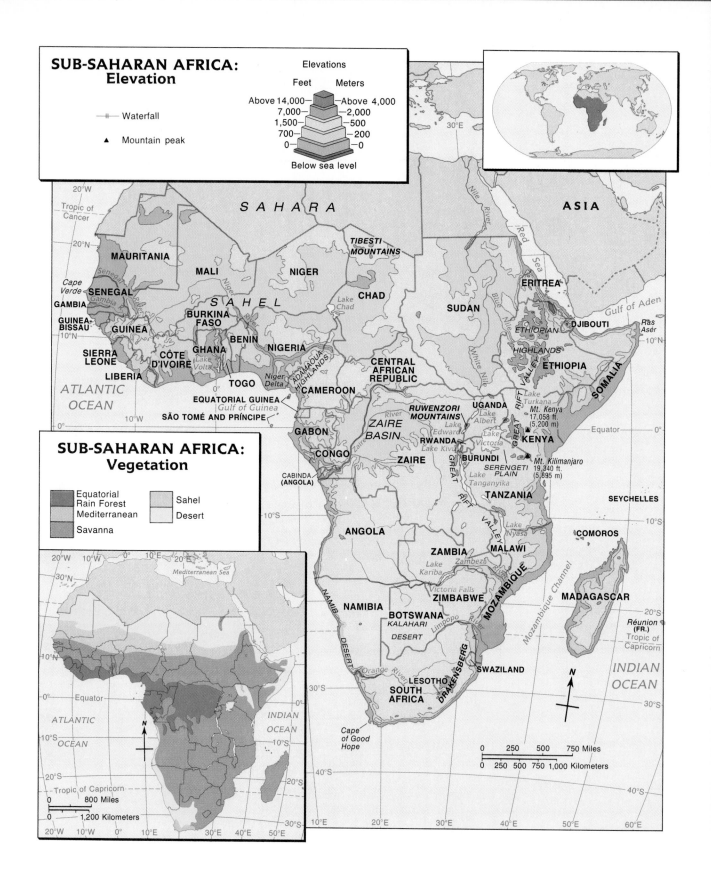

SUB-SAHARAN AFRICA: Elevation

Elevations

Feet	Meters
Above 14,000	Above 4,000
7,000	2,000
1,500	500
700	200
0	0

Below sea level

—╫— Waterfall

▲ Mountain peak

SUB-SAHARAN AFRICA: Vegetation

- Equatorial Rain Forest
- Mediterranean
- Savanna
- Sahel
- Desert

SAHARA

TIBESTI MOUNTAINS

ASIA

Tropic of Cancer

20°W

20°N

MAURITANIA

MALI

NIGER

CHAD

SUDAN

ERITREA

Red Sea

Gulf of Aden

DJIBOUTI

Ras Asér

Cape Verde

SENEGAL

Lake Chad

Nile River

30°E

GAMBIA

Senegal

Gambia

GUINEA-BISSAU

GUINEA

BURKINA FASO

SAHEL

Niger River

ETHIOPIAN HIGHLANDS

Blue Nile

White Nile

ETHIOPIA

10°N

SIERRA LEONE

LIBERIA

CÔTE D'IVOIRE

GHANA

Lake Volta

BENIN

TOGO

NIGERIA

ADAMAOUA HIGHLANDS

Niger Delta

CENTRAL AFRICAN REPUBLIC

SOMALIA

ATLANTIC OCEAN

10°W

0°

EQUATORIAL GUINEA

Gulf of Guinea

SÃO TOMÉ AND PRÍNCIPE

CAMEROON

RUWENZORI MOUNTAINS

River

UGANDA

Lake Albert

Mt. Kenya 17,058 ft. (5,200 m) ▲

KENYA

Equator

0°

GABON

ZAIRE BASIN

Lake Edward

RWANDA

Lake Victoria

CONGO

ZAIRE

BURUNDI

Lake Kivu

GREAT RIFT VALLEY

Mt. Kilimanjaro 19,340 ft. (5,895 m)

SERENGETI PLAIN

SEYCHELLES

CABINDA (ANGOLA)

Lake Tanganyika

TANZANIA

10°S

GREAT RIFT VALLEY

Lake Nyasa

COMOROS

ANGOLA

ZAMBIA

Lake Kariba

Zambezi

MALAWI

MADAGASCAR

NAMIB

NAMIBIA

BOTSWANA

KALAHARI DESERT

ZIMBABWE

Victoria Falls

MOZAMBIQUE

Limpopo River

Mozambique Channel

Réunion (FR.)

Tropic of Capricorn

20°S

DESERT

Orange River

SWAZILAND

N

INDIAN OCEAN

Cape of Good Hope

LESOTHO

SOUTH AFRICA

DRAKENSBERG

30°S

| 0 | 250 | 500 | 750 Miles |
| 0 | 250 500 750 | 1,000 Kilometers |

40°S

Vegetation inset:

20°W 10°W 0° 10°E 20°E 30°N

Mediterranean Sea

10°N

0° Equator

ATLANTIC OCEAN

INDIAN OCEAN

10°S

N

20°S

Tropic of Capricorn

| 0 | 800 Miles |
| 0 | 1,200 Kilometers |

30°S

20°W 10°W 0° 10°E 20°E 30°E 40°E 50°E

DESERT SURFACES OF THE SAHARA

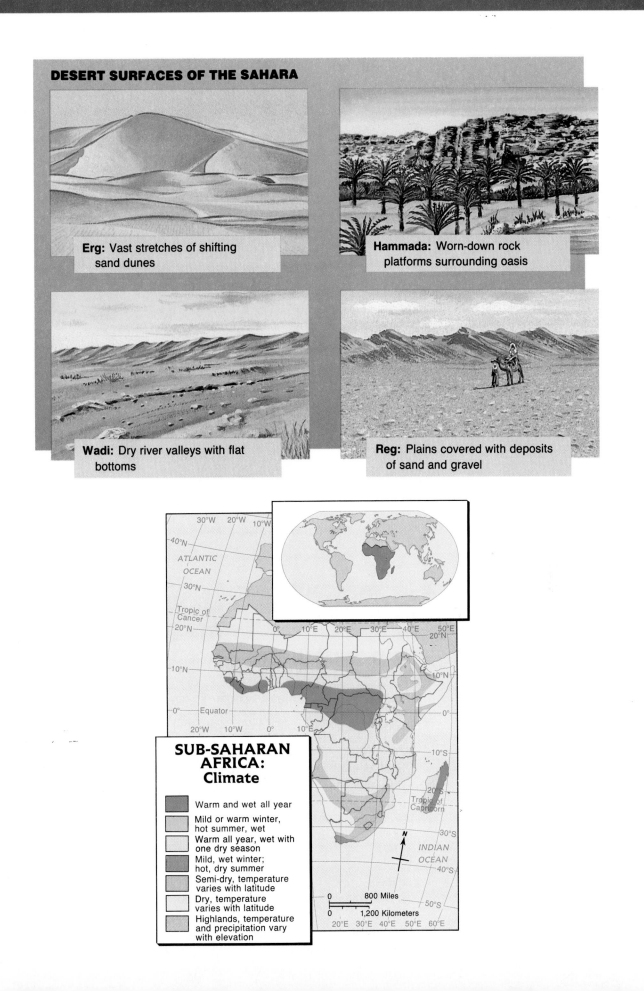

Erg: Vast stretches of shifting sand dunes

Hammada: Worn-down rock platforms surrounding oasis

Wadi: Dry river valleys with flat bottoms

Reg: Plains covered with deposits of sand and gravel

SUB-SAHARAN AFRICA: Climate

- Warm and wet all year
- Mild or warm winter, hot summer, wet
- Warm all year, wet with one dry season
- Mild, wet winter; hot, dry summer
- Semi-dry, temperature varies with latitude
- Dry, temperature varies with latitude
- Highlands, temperature and precipitation vary with elevation

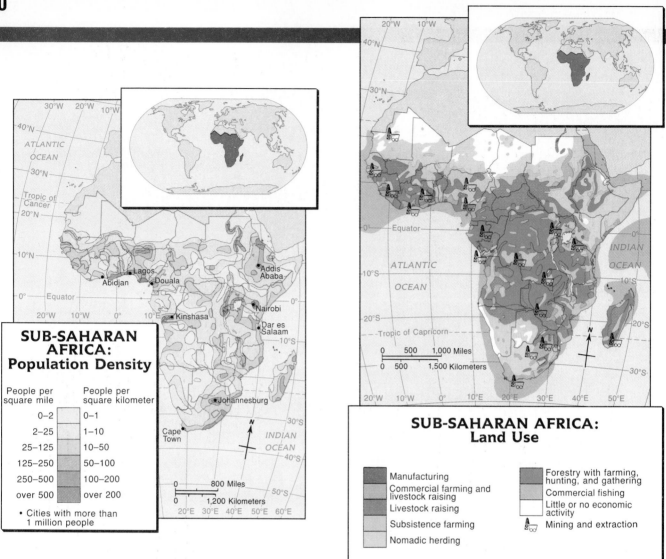

SUB-SAHARAN AFRICA: Population Density

People per square mile	People per square kilometer
0–2	0–1
2–25	1–10
25–125	10–50
125–250	50–100
250–500	100–200
over 500	over 200

• Cities with more than 1 million people

SUB-SAHARAN AFRICA: Land Use

- Manufacturing
- Commercial farming and livestock raising
- Livestock raising
- Subsistence farming
- Nomadic herding
- Forestry with farming, hunting, and gathering
- Commercial fishing
- Little or no economic activity
- Mining and extraction

SUB-SAHARAN AFRICA

Country	Capital	Area in sq mi (sq km)	Population
Angola	Luanda	481,352 (1,246,700)	8,500,000
Benin	Porto-Novo	43,483 (112,620)	4,800,000
Botswana	Gaborone	231,803 (600,370)	1,300,000
Burkina Faso	Ouagadougou	105,869 (274,200)	9,400,000
Burundi	Bujumbura	10,745 (27,830)	5,800,000
Cameroon	Yaoundé	183,568 (475,440)	11,400,000
Cape Verde	Praia	1,556 (4,030)	400,000
Central African Republic	Bangui	237,362 (622,980)	3,000,000
Chad	N'Djamena	495,754 (1,284,000)	5,100,000
Comoros	Moroni	838 (2,170)	500,000
Congo	Brazzaville	132,047 (342,000)	2,300,000

Country	Capital	Area in sq mi (sq km)	Population
Côte d'Ivoire	Yamoussoukro	124,502 (322,460)	12,500,000
Djibouti	Djibouti	8,494 (22,000)	400,000
Equatorial Guinea	Malabo	10,830 (28,050)	400,000
Eritrea	Asmara	36,170 (93,679)	3,300,000
Ethiopia	Addis Ababa	435,607 (1,128,221)	50,500,000
Gabon	Libreville	103,348 (267,670)	1,200,000
Gambia, (The)	Banjul	4,363 (11,300)	900,000
Ghana	Accra	92,101 (238,540)	15,500,000
Guinea	Conakry	94,927 (245,860)	7,500,000
Guinea-Bissau	Bissau	13,946 (36,120)	1,000,000
Kenya	Nairobi	224,962 (582,650)	25,200,000
Lesotho	Maseru	11,718 (30,350)	1,800,000
Liberia	Monrovia	43,000 (111,370)	2,700,000
Madagascar	Antananarivo	226,656 (587,040)	12,400,000
Malawi	Lilongwe	45,745 (118,480)	9,400,000
Mali	Bamako	478,765 (1,240,000)	8,300,000
Mauritania	Nouakchott	397,954 (1,030,700)	2,100,000
Mauritius	Port Louis	718 (1,860)	1,100,000
Mozambique	Maputo	309,495 (801,590)	16,100,000
Namibia	Windhoek	318,259 (824,290)	1,500,000
Niger	Niamey	489,190 (1,267,000)	8,000,000
Nigeria	Abuja	356,669 (923,770)	122,500,000
Rwanda	Kigali	10,170 (26,340)	7,500,000
São Tomé and Príncipe	São Tomé	371 (960)	100,000
Senegal	Dakar	75,749 (196,190)	7,500,000
Seychelles	Victoria	171 (443)	100,000
Sierra Leone	Freetown	27,699 (71,740)	4,300,000
Somalia	Mogadishu	246,201 (637,660)	7,700,000
South Africa	Pretoria; Cape Town; Bloemfontein	471,445 (1,221,040)	40,600,000
Sudan	Khartoum	967,496 (2,505,810)	25,900,000
Swaziland	Mbabane	6,703 (17,360)	800,000
Tanzania	Dar es Salaam	364,900 (945,090)	26,900,000
Togo	Lomé	21,927 (56,790)	3,800,000
Uganda	Kampala	91,135 (236,040)	18,700,000
Zaire	Kinshasa	905,565 (2,345,410)	37,800,000
Zambia	Lusaka	290,583 (752,610)	8,400,000
Zimbabwe	Harare	150,803 (390,580)	10,000,000

SOUTHERN AND EASTERN ASIA

The continent of Asia is divided into three sections. Northern Asia includes Russia and its neighbors. (You can see maps of this area on pages 42–46.) Western Asia is the area many know as the Middle East. The rest of the continent makes up the world's largest region, known as Southern and Eastern Asia. Here are the world's tallest mountains, some of the world's longest rivers, thousands of islands—and millions upon millions of people.

The region of Southern and Eastern Asia is the most populated in the world. More than one half of the world's people

Southern and Eastern Asia is home to people of many different cultures.

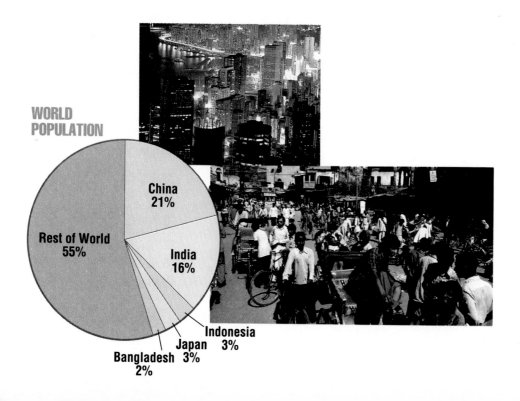

WORLD POPULATION

- China 21%
- Rest of World 55%
- India 16%
- Indonesia 3%
- Japan 3%
- Bangladesh 2%

live here, although the region contains less than one fifth of all the land on the earth. China alone houses over one billion people, or about one fifth of the world's population. India is only about one third the size of the United States, but it contains 859 million people—more than three times the number of people that live in the United States!

As you look at the maps of this region, think about what it would take to meet the basic needs of over one billion people. Judging from the maps of Southern and Eastern Asia, conclude how well equipped this region is to meet the needs and wants of all its people.

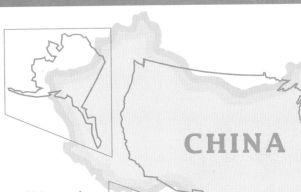

China and the United States are about the same size in land area.

China's Great Wall is 1,500 miles (2,200 km) long. It is the only human-made object that can be seen from space.

People in Nepal raise crops and animals in the awesome shadow of Mount Everest, the world's tallest mountain.

Farmers in Southern Asia depend on summer rains to water their crops.

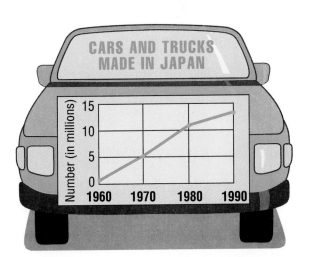

Over the past 30 years, Japan has become a world leader in the production of cars and trucks. According to the graph, between what years did Japan's production grow the most?

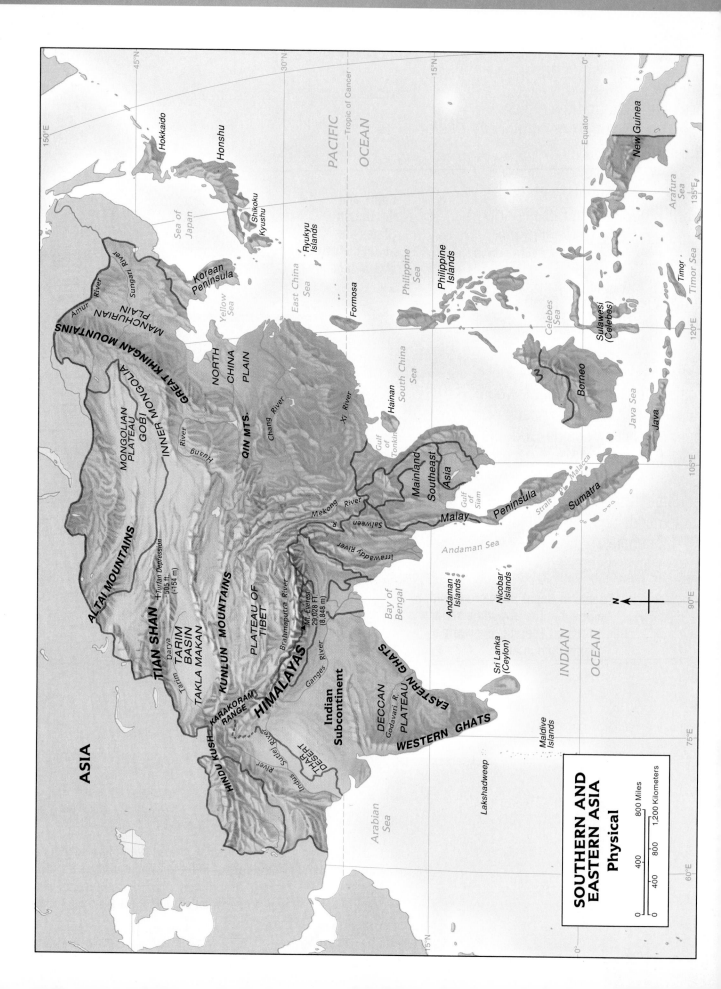

SOUTHERN AND EASTERN ASIA
Physical

ASIA

ALTAI MOUNTAINS
TIAN SHAN
TARIM BASIN
Darya
Tarim
TAKLA MAKAN
Turfan Depression
-505 ft.
(-154 m)
KUNLUN MOUNTAINS
MONGOLIAN PLATEAU
GOBI
INNER MONGOLIA
GREAT KHINGAN MOUNTAINS
MANCHURIAN PLAIN
Amur River
Sungari River
Huang River

HINDU KUSH
KARAKORAM RANGE
PLATEAU OF TIBET
HIMALAYAS
Mt. Everest
29,028 FT.
(8,848 m)
Brahmaputra River
Ganges River
Sutlej River
Indus River
THAR DESERT
Indian Subcontinent
DECCAN PLATEAU
Godavari R.
WESTERN GHATS
EASTERN GHATS

QIN MTS.
NORTH CHINA PLAIN
Chang River
Xi River
Hainan
Mekong River
Salween R.
Irrawaddy River
Mainland Southeast Asia
Gulf of Tonkin
Gulf of Siam
Malay Peninsula
Strait of Malacca

Korean Peninsula
Hokkaido
Honshu
Shikoku
Kyushu
Sea of Japan
Yellow Sea
East China Sea
Ryukyu Islands
Formosa
South China Sea
Philippine Sea
Philippine Islands
PACIFIC OCEAN
Tropic of Cancer
Equator
New Guinea
Arafura Sea
Timor
Timor Sea
Java Sea
Java
Sumatra
Borneo
Celebes Sea
Sulawesi (Celebes)

Andaman Sea
Andaman Islands
Nicobar Islands
Bay of Bengal
Sri Lanka (Ceylon)
INDIAN OCEAN
Maldive Islands
Lakshadweep
Arabian Sea

N

800 Miles
400
0
1,200 Kilometers
800
400
0

45°N
30°N
15°N
15°S

150°E
135°E
120°E
105°E
90°E
75°E
60°E

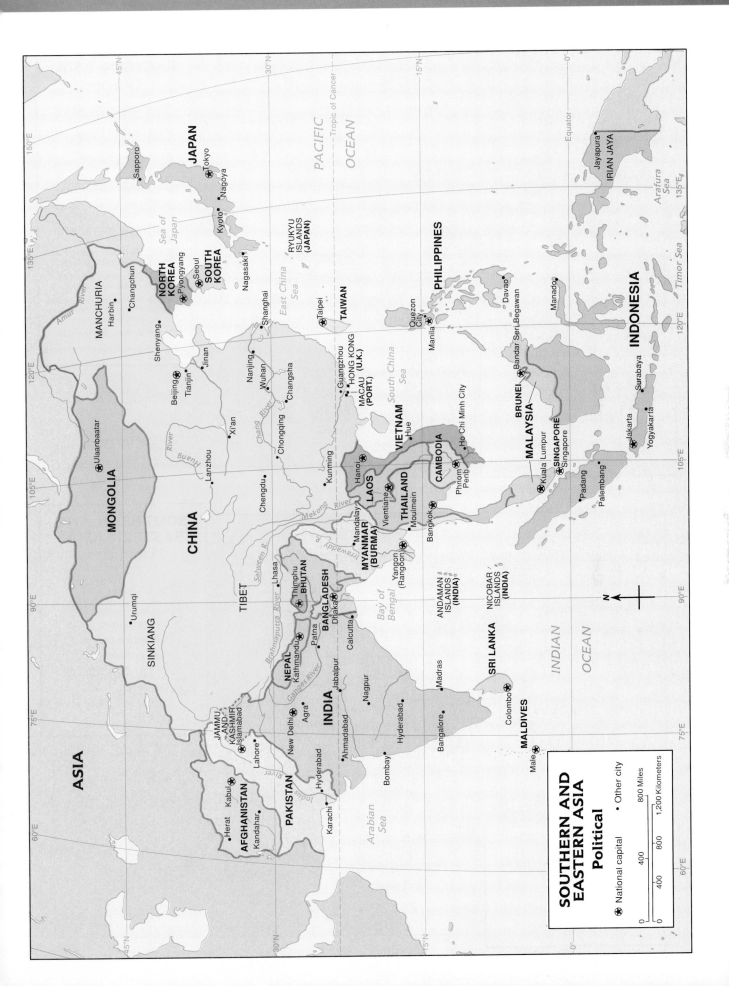

ASIA

JAPAN
Sapporo•
•Tokyo
Kyoto• •Nagoya

MANCHURIA
•Changchun
Harbin•

NORTH KOREA
Pyongyang⊛ •Seoul
SOUTH KOREA
•Nagasaki

RYUKYU ISLANDS (JAPAN)

PACIFIC OCEAN

Tropic of Cancer

Equator

IRIAN JAYA
•Jayapura

Arafura Sea

135°E

MONGOLIA
Ulaanbaatar⊛

Urumqi•

SINKIANG

CHINA

Shenyang•
Beijing⊛ •Tianjin
Jinan•
Xi'an•
Nanjing• •Shanghai
Wuhan• •Changsha
Lanzhou•
Chengdu•
Chongqing•

Amur River

Sea of Japan

East China Sea

Shanghai

Huang River

Chang River

Kunming•

Guangzhou•
HONG KONG (U.K.)
MACAU (PORT.)

South China Sea

Taipei⊛
TAIWAN

PHILIPPINES
Quezon City
Manila⊛
•Davao

INDONESIA
•Manado

120°E

TIBET
Lhasa•

Thimphu⊛
BHUTAN
Kathmandu⊛
NEPAL
Patna•
BANGLADESH
Dhaka⊛
Jabalpur•
Calcutta•

Brahmaputra River

Ganges River

Salween R.

Mekong River

Irrawaddy R.

MYANMAR (BURMA)
Mandalay•
Yangon (Rangoon)⊛

LAOS
Hanoi⊛
Vientiane⊛

VIETNAM
Hue•
Ho Chi Minh City•

THAILAND
Moulmein•
Bangkok⊛

CAMBODIA
Phnom Penh⊛

BRUNEI
Bandar Seri Begawan⊛

MALAYSIA
Kuala Lumpur⊛
SINGAPORE
Singapore⊛

Padang•
Palembang•

Jakarta⊛
Surabaya•
Yogyakarta•

105°E

ANDAMAN ISLANDS (INDIA)

NICOBAR ISLANDS (INDIA)

Bay of Bengal

INDIAN OCEAN

Timor Sea

90°E

AFGHANISTAN
Herat• •Kabul
Kandahar•

PAKISTAN
Islamabad⊛
Lahore•
Hyderabad•
Karachi•

JAMMU AND KASHMIR

Indus River

New Delhi⊛
Agra•
Ahmadabad•
INDIA
Nagpur•
Bombay•
Hyderabad•
Bangalore•
Madras•

SRI LANKA
Colombo⊛

MALDIVES
Male⊛

Arabian Sea

75°E

60°E

45°N

30°N

15°N

Equator

N

SOUTHERN AND EASTERN ASIA
Political

⊛ National capital   • Other city

0   400   800 Miles
0   400   800   1,200 Kilometers

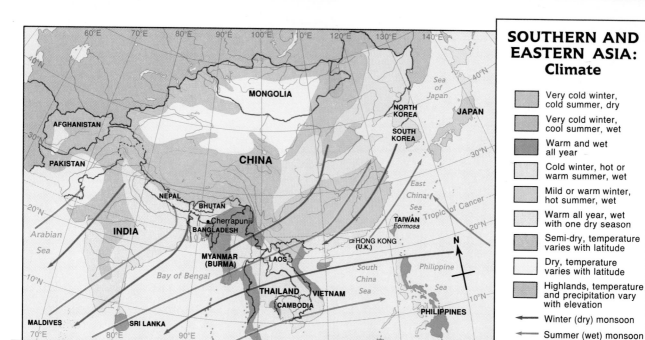

SOUTHERN AND EASTERN ASIA: Climate

- Very cold winter, cold summer, dry
- Very cold winter, cool summer, wet
- Warm and wet all year
- Cold winter, hot or warm summer, wet
- Mild or warm winter, hot summer, wet
- Warm all year, wet with one dry season
- Semi-dry, temperature varies with latitude
- Dry, temperature varies with latitude
- Highlands, temperature and precipitation vary with elevation
- ⟵ Winter (dry) monsoon
- ⟵ Summer (wet) monsoon

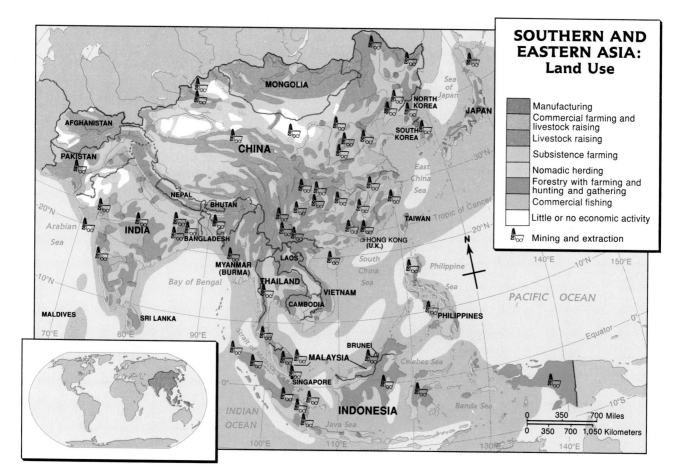

SOUTHERN AND EASTERN ASIA: Land Use

- Manufacturing
- Commercial farming and livestock raising
- Livestock raising
- Subsistence farming
- Nomadic herding
- Forestry with farming and hunting and gathering
- Commercial fishing
- Little or no economic activity
- ⛏ Mining and extraction

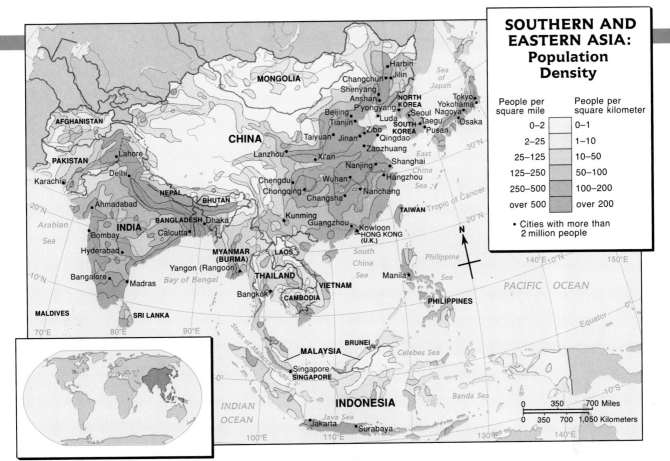

SOUTHERN AND EASTERN ASIA: Population Density

People per square mile	People per square kilometer
0–2	0–1
2–25	1–10
25–125	10–50
125–250	50–100
250–500	100–200
over 500	over 200

• Cities with more than 2 million people

SOUTHERN AND EASTERN ASIA

Country	Capital	Area in sq mi (sq km)	Population
Afghanistan	Kabul	251,773 (647,500)	16,600,000
Bangladesh	Dhaka	55,599 (144,000)	116,600,000
Bhutan	Thimphu	18,147 (47,000)	700,000
Brunei	Bandar Seri Begawan	2,228 (5,770)	300,000
Cambodia	Phnom Penh	69,900 (181,040)	7,100,000
China	Beijing	3,705,396 (9,596,960)	1,151,300,000
India	New Delhi	1,269,342 (3,287,590)	859,200,000
Indonesia	Jakarta	741,098 (1,919,440)	181,400,000
Japan	Tokyo	143,749 (372,310)	123,800,000
Korea, North	Pyongyang	46,541 (120,540)	21,800,000
Korea, South	Seoul	38,023 (98,480)	43,200,000
Laos	Vientiane	91,429 (236,800)	4,100,000
Malaysia	Kuala Lumpur	127,317 (329,750)	18,300,000
Maldives	Malé	116 (300)	200,000
Mongolia	Ulaanbaatar	604,248 (1,565,000)	2,200,000
Myanmar (Burma)	Yangon (Rangoon)	261,217 (676,550)	42,100,000
Nepal	Kathmandu	54,363 (140,800)	19,600,000
Pakistan	Islamabad	310,402 (803,940)	117,500,000
Philippines	Manila	115,830 (300,000)	62,300,000
Singapore	Singapore	224 (580)	2,800,000
Sri Lanka	Colombo	25,332 (65,610)	17,400,000
Taiwan	Taipei	13,892 (35,980)	20,500,000
Thailand	Bangkok	198,456 (514,000)	58,800,000
Vietnam	Hanoi	127,243 (329,560)	67,600,000

THE PACIFIC

As in every region, young people are the Pacific region's most precious resource.

What do you suppose it would be like to live on a small island in the middle of an ocean? In what ways would it be different from living in the middle of a big country like the United States?

Island living is a way of life for people in the Pacific region, which is made up of thousands of islands in the Pacific Ocean and the continents of Australia and Antarctica. Some people live on tiny islands that are hundreds of miles away from each other. Many others live on the con-

WORLD'S FRESHWATER SUPPLY

Other 30%

Antarctica 70%

According to the graph, what percentage of the world's freshwater supply is located in Antarctica?

Antarctica's icy landscape is home to penguins—but not polar bears. As the drawing shows, polar bears live only near the North Pole.

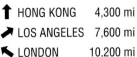

→	NEW ZEALAND	1,600 mi
↑	HONG KONG	4,300 mi
↘	LOS ANGELES	7,600 mi
↖	LONDON	10,200 mi

Australia

tinent of Australia, which is hardly a tiny island but is still isolated by miles of ocean from its nearest neighbor.

The mighty Pacific Ocean is the tie that binds the people and lands of this region together. As you look at the maps in this section, think about how the Pacific Ocean helps to provide the basic needs of the people in this region. Then think about how it limits the way people in the Pacific region live.

Many Australians live on isolated farms and ranches. Some young people even "go to school" by radio because they live too far away from the nearest school.

This island, like many in the Pacific region, is made of coral.

In New Zealand, sheep outnumber people by 20 to 1.

Ayers Rock towers above the desert-like Australian outback.

The Sydney Opera House is one of the most famous landmarks in Australia.

The Pacific region is located within the "Ring of Fire," the volcanic chain that rims the Pacific Ocean. Most of the world's volcanoes are found along this chain.

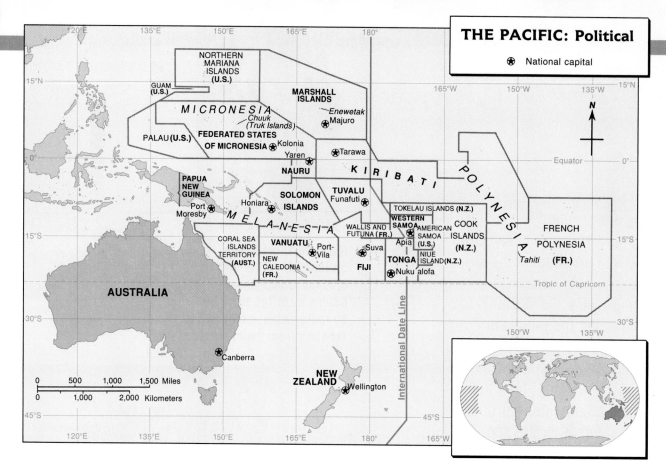

THE PACIFIC

Country	Capital	Area in sq mi (sq km)	Population
Australia	Canberra	2,967,900 (7,686,850)	17,500,000
Fiji	Suva	7,054 (18,270)	700,000
Kiribati	Tarawa	277 (717)	71,000
Marshall Islands	Majuro	70 (113)	43,000
Micronesia, Fed. States	Kolonia	270 (700)	107,662
Nauru	Yaren	8 (20)	8,100
New Zealand	Wellington	103,738 (268,680)	3,500,000
Papua New Guinea	Port Moresby	178,259 (461,690)	3,900,000
Solomon Islands	Honiara	10,985 (28,450)	300,000
Tonga	Nuku'alofa	270 (700)	102,000
Tuvalu	Funafuti	10 (26)	9,000
Vanuatu	Port-Vila	5,699 (14,760)	200,000
Western Samoa	Apia	1,104 (2,860)	200,000

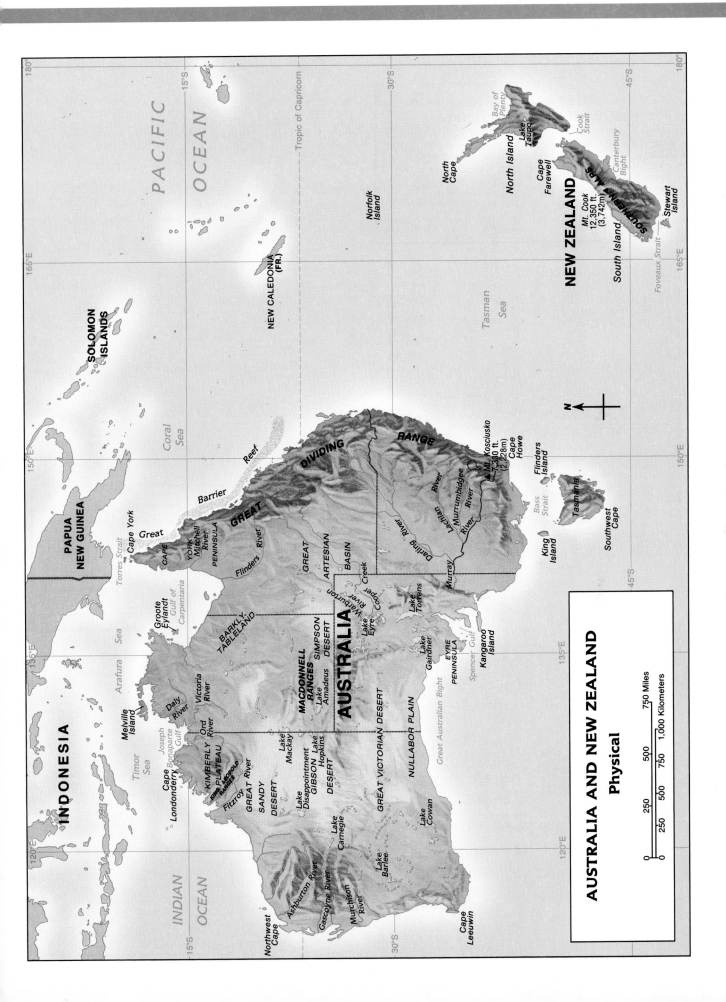

AUSTRALIA AND NEW ZEALAND
Physical

PACIFIC OCEAN

INDONESIA

PAPUA NEW GUINEA

SOLOMON ISLANDS

NEW CALEDONIA (FR.)

Norfolk Island

NEW ZEALAND

North Cape
North Island
Bay of Plenty
Lake Taupo
Cook Strait
Cape Farewell
SOUTHERN ALPS
Mt. Cook 12,350 ft. (3,742m)
South Island
Canterbury Bight
Stewart Island
Foveaux Strait

Tasman Sea

AUSTRALIA

Coral Sea
Barrier Reef
Great Barrier Reef
Cape York
YORK PENINSULA
CAPE
Mitchell River
Flinders River
GREAT DIVIDING RANGE
GREAT ARTESIAN BASIN
Warburton River
Cooper Creek
Darling River
Lachlan River
Murrumbidgee River
Murray River
Mt. Kosciusko 7,330 ft. (2,228m)
Cape Howe
Flinders Island
Bass Strait
Tasmania
King Island
Southwest Cape

Torres Strait
Gulf of Carpentaria
Groote Eylandt
BARKLY TABLELAND
SIMPSON DESERT
MACDONNELL RANGES
Lake Amadeus
Lake Eyre
Lake Torrens
EYRE PENINSULA
Lake Gairdner
Spencer Gulf
Kangaroo Island
Great Australian Bight

Arafura Sea
Melville Island
Cape Londonderry
Cape Joseph Bonaparte Gulf
Timor Sea
Daly River
Ord River
Victoria River
KIMBERLY PLATEAU
KING LEOPOLD RANGES
Fitzroy River
GREAT SANDY DESERT
Lake Mackay
Lake Disappointment
GIBSON DESERT
Lake Hopkins
GREAT VICTORIAN DESERT
NULLABOR PLAIN
Lake Carnegie
Lake Barlee
Lake Cowan

INDIAN OCEAN
Northwest Cape
Ashburton River
Gascoyne River
Murchison River
Cape Leeuwin

N

0 250 500 750 Miles
0 250 500 750 1,000 Kilometers

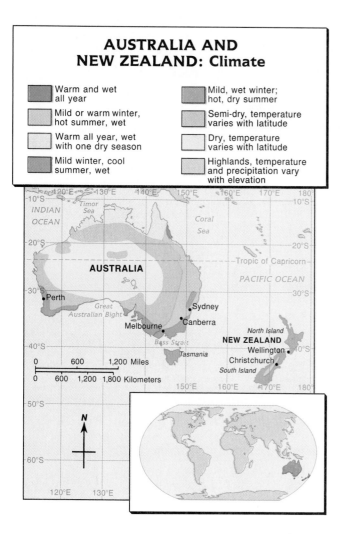

AUSTRALIA AND NEW ZEALAND: Climate

- Warm and wet all year
- Mild or warm winter, hot summer, wet
- Warm all year, wet with one dry season
- Mild winter, cool summer, wet
- Mild, wet winter; hot, dry summer
- Semi-dry, temperature varies with latitude
- Dry, temperature varies with latitude
- Highlands, temperature and precipitation vary with elevation

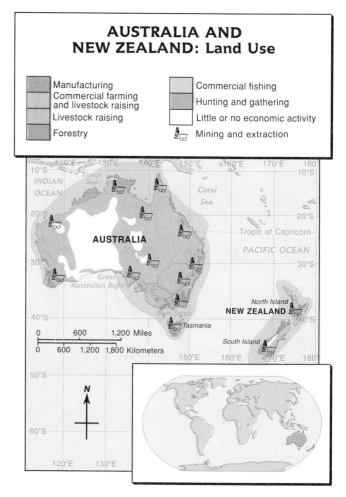

AUSTRALIA AND NEW ZEALAND: Land Use

- Manufacturing
- Commercial farming and livestock raising
- Livestock raising
- Forestry
- Commercial fishing
- Hunting and gathering
- Little or no economic activity
- Mining and extraction

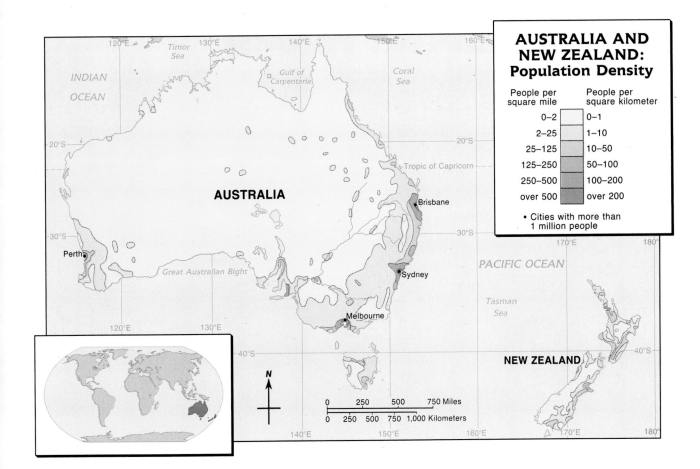

AUSTRALIA AND NEW ZEALAND: Population Density

People per square mile	People per square kilometer
0–2	0–1
2–25	1–10
25–125	10–50
125–250	50–100
250–500	100–200
over 500	over 200

• Cities with more than 1 million people

INDIAN OCEAN

Timor Sea

Gulf of Carpentaria

Coral Sea

AUSTRALIA

Tropic of Capricorn

Brisbane

Perth

Great Australian Bight

Sydney

Melbourne

PACIFIC OCEAN

Tasman Sea

NEW ZEALAND

N

| 0 | 250 | 500 | 750 Miles |
| 0 | 250 | 500 | 750 | 1,000 Kilometers |

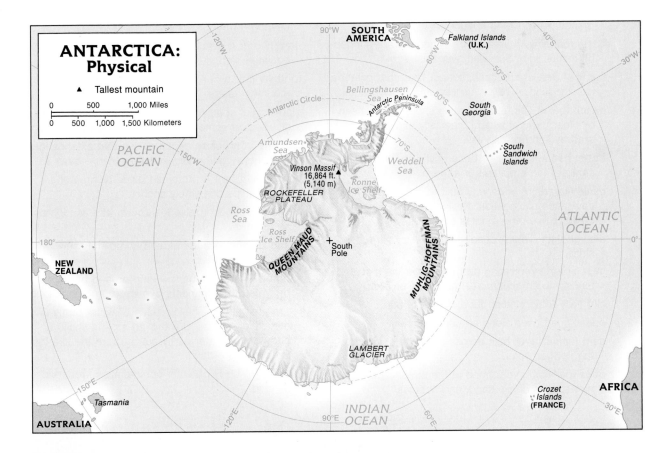

ANTARCTICA: Physical

▲ Tallest mountain

| 0 | 500 | 1,000 Miles |
| 0 | 500 | 1,000 | 1,500 Kilometers |

SOUTH AMERICA

Falkland Islands (U.K.)

Bellingshausen Sea

Antarctic Circle

Antarctic Peninsula

South Georgia

PACIFIC OCEAN

Amundsen Sea

Vinson Massif 16,864 ft. (5,140 m)

ROCKEFELLER PLATEAU

Ronne Ice Shelf

Weddell Sea

South Sandwich Islands

ATLANTIC OCEAN

Ross Sea

Ross Ice Shelf

QUEEN MAUD MOUNTAINS

South Pole

MUHLIG-HOFFMAN MOUNTAINS

NEW ZEALAND

LAMBERT GLACIER

AFRICA

Tasmania

Crozet Islands (FRANCE)

AUSTRALIA

INDIAN OCEAN

74

DICTIONARY OF
GEOGRAPHIC TERMS

volcano

river basin

hill

lake

basin

reservoir

dune

desert

plain

dam

beach

oasis

gulf

reef

cliff

delta

atoll

archipelago

island

lagoon

ocean (sea)

archipelago (är kə pel′ ə gō) A large group or chain of islands.

atoll (āt′ ôl) A ring-shaped coral island or string of islands, surrounding a lagoon.

basin (bā′ sin) An area of low-lying land surrounded by higher land. *See also* **river basin.**

bay (bā) Part of an ocean, sea, or lake, that extends into the land. A bay is usually smaller than a gulf.

beach (bēch) The gently sloping shore of an ocean or other body of water, especially that part covered by sand or pebbles.

butte (būt) A small, flat-topped hill. A butte is smaller than a plateau or a mesa.

canal (kə nal′) A waterway built to carry water for navigation or irrigation. Navigation canals usually connect two other bodies of water.

canyon (kan′ yən) A deep, narrow valley with steep sides.

cape (kāp) A projecting part of a coastline that extends into an ocean, sea, gulf, bay, or lake.

cliff (klif) A high, steep face of rock or earth.

coast (kōst) Land along an ocean or sea.

dam (dam) A wall built across a river to hold back the flowing water.

delta (del′ tə) Land formed at the mouth of a river by deposits of silt, sand, and pebbles.

desert (dez′ ərt) A very dry area where few plants grow.

dune (dün) A mound, hill, or ridge of sand that is heaped up by the wind.

fjord (fyôrd) A deep, narrow inlet of the sea between high, steep cliffs.

foothills (fut′ hilz) A hilly area at the base of a mountain range.

glacier (glā′ shər) A large sheet of ice that moves slowly over some land surface or down a valley.

gulf (gulf) Part of an ocean or sea that extends into the land. A gulf is usually larger than a bay.

harbor (här′ bər) A protected place along a shore where ships can safely anchor.

hill (hil) A rounded, raised landform, not as high as a mountain.

island (ī′ lənd) A body of land completely surrounded by water.

isthmus (is′ məs) A narrow strip of land bordered by water, that connects two larger bodies of land.

lagoon (lə gün′) A shallow body of water partly or completely enclosed within an atoll; a shallow body of sea water partly cut off from the sea by a narrow strip of land.

lake (lāk) A body of water completely surrounded by land.

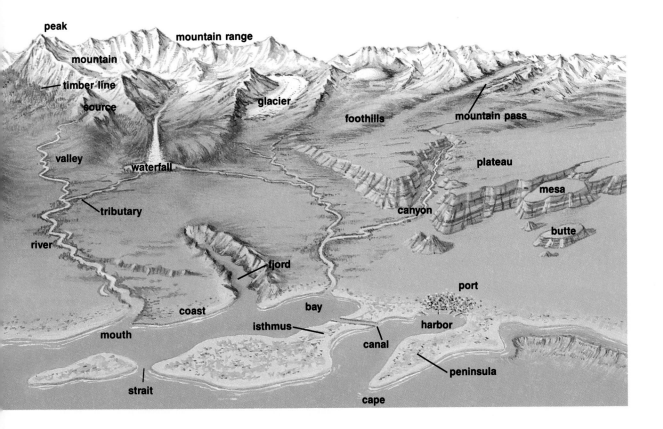

mesa (mā′ sə) A high, flat landform rising steeply above the surrounding land. A mesa is smaller than a plateau and larger than a butte.

mountain (mount′ ən) A high, rounded or pointed landform with steep sides, higher than a hill.

mountain pass (mount′ ən pas) An opening or gap through a mountain range.

mountain range (mount′ ən rānj) A row or chain of mountains.

mouth (mouth) The place where a river empties into another body of water.

oasis (ō ā′ sis) A place in the desert made fertile by a steady supply of water.

ocean (ō′ shən) One of the earth's four largest bodies of water. The four oceans are really a single connected body of salt water that covers about three fourths of the earth's surface.

peak (pēk) The pointed top of a mountain or hill.

peninsula (pə nin′ sə lə) A body of land nearly surrounded by water.

plain (plān) A large area of flat or nearly flat land.

plateau (pla tō′) A high, flat landform that rises steeply above the surrounding land. A plateau is larger than a mesa and a butte.

port (pôrt) A place where ships load and unload goods.

reef (rēf) A ridge of sand, rock, or coral that lies at or near the surface of a sea.

reservoir (rez′ ər vwär) A natural or artificial lake used to store water.

river (riv′ ər) A large stream of water that flows across the land and usually empties into a lake, ocean, or other river.

river basin (riv′ ər bās′ in) All the land drained by a river and its tributaries.

sea (sē) A large body of water partly or entirely surrounded by land; another word for *ocean*.

source (sôrs) The place where a river or stream begins.

strait (strāt) A narrow waterway or channel connecting two larger bodies of water.

timber line (tim′ bər līn) An imaginary line on mountains, above which trees do not grow.

tributary (trib′ yə târ ē) A river or stream that flows into a larger river or stream.

valley (val′ ē) An area of low land between hills or mountains.

volcano (vol kā′ nō) An opening in the earth through which lava, rock, gases, and ash are forced out.

waterfall (wô′ tər fôl) A flow of water falling from a high place to a lower place.

GAZETTEER

This Gazetteer is a geographical dictionary that will help you to pronounce and locate the places shown in this Atlas. Latitude and longitude are given for cities and some other places. The page number tells you where each place appears on a regional map for the first time.

PRONUNCIATION KEY

a	cap	êr	clear	oi	coin	ü	moon
ā	cake	hw	where	ôr	fork	ū	cute
ä	father	i	bib	ou	cow	ûr	term
är	car	ī	kite	sh	show	ə	about, taken
âr	dare	ng	song	th	thin		pencil, apron,
ch	chain	o	top	th	those		helpful
e	hen	ō	rope	u	sun	ər	letter, dollar,
ē	me	ô	saw	ù	book		doctor

A

Abidjan (ab i jän′) The largest city of Côte d'Ivoire; 5°N, 4°W. (p. 60)

Abu Dhabi (ä bü dä′ bē) The capital of the United Arab Emirates; 25°N, 55°E. (p. 51)

Abuja (ä bu′ jə) The capital of Nigeria; 6°N, 3°E. (p. 57)

Accra (ə krä′) The capital and largest city of Ghana; 5°N, 1°W. (p. 57)

Addis Ababa (ad′ is ab′ ə bə) The capital and largest city of Ethiopia; 9°N, 38°E. (p. 57)

Adelaide (ad′ ə lād) A city in southern Australia; 138°E, 35°S. (p. 71)

Afghanistan (af gan′ ə stan) A country in south-central Asia. Capital, Kabul. (p. 65)

Africa (af′ ri kə) The world's second-largest continent. It lies between the Atlantic and Indian oceans. (p. 3)

Ahaggar Mountains (ə häg′ ər moun′ tənz) A mountainous region in the central Sahara in Africa. (p. 50)

Ahmadabad (ä mə də bäd′) A city in west-central India; 26°N, 73°E. (p. 65)

Alabama (al ə bam′ ə) A state in the southeastern United States. Capital, Montgomery. (p. 15)

Alaska (ə las′ kə) The largest state of the United States, on the extreme northwestern peninsula of North America. Capital, Juneau. (p. 15)

Alaska Range (ə las′ kə rānj) A mountain range stretching across southern Alaska. (p. 14)

Albania (al bā′ nē ə) A country in southeastern Europe, on the Balkan Peninsula. Capital, Tiranë. (p. 43)

Albany (ôl′ bə nē) The capital of New York; 42°N, 70°W. (p. 15)

Alexandria (al ig zan′ drē ə) A port city in Egypt; 2°N, 30°E. (p. 51)

Algeria (al jîr′ ē ə) A country in northern Africa, on the Mediterranean Sea. Capital, Algiers. (p. 51)

Algiers (al jîrz′) The capital of Algeria; 36°N, 3°E. (p.51)

Allegheny River (al i gā′ nē riv′ ər) A river in western Pennsylvania and in southwestern New York. Length, 325 miles (523 km). (p. 22)

Alma-Ata (al′ mə a′ tä) The capital of Kazakhstan; 44°N, 77°E. (p. 43)

Alps (alps) A major European mountain system, extending in an arc from the Mediterranean coast east to the Balkan Peninsula. (p. 42)

Altai Mountains (al′ tī moun′ tənz) A mountain range in Asia, extending from the south-central part of Russia east into western Mongolia. (p. 42)

Amazon River (am′ ə zon riv′ ər) The longest river in South America and the second-longest river in the world. Length, 4,000 miles (6,400 km). (p. 34)

American Samoa (ə mer′ i kən sə mō′ ə) An island group in the Pacific Ocean, a territory of the United States. Capital, Pago Pago. (p. 71)

Amman (ä män′) The capital of Jordan; 31°N, 35°E. (p. 51)

Amsterdam (am′ stər dam) The capital and largest city of the Netherlands; 52°N, 4°E. (p. 43)

Amu Darya (ä mü där′ yə) A river in central Asia, flowing into the Aral Sea. Length, 1,578 miles (2,545 km). (p. 42)

Amur River (ä mür′ riv′ ər) A river in northeastern Asia, forming part of the boundary between Russia and China. Length, 2,744 miles (4,390 km). (p. 42)

Anadyr′ Range (än ə dir′ rānj) An extension of the Kolyma Mountains, near the Arctic Circle in Russia. (p. 42)

Andaman Islands (an′ də mən ī′ ləndz) A group of islands located in the Andaman Sea. (p. 65)

Andaman Sea (an′ də mən sē) The northeastern part of the Indian Ocean, lying between India and the Malay Peninsula. (p. 64)

Andes Mountains (an′ dēz moun′ tənz) The longest mountain chain in the world, stretching along the west coast of South America. (p. 34)

Andorra (an dôr′ ə) A country in southwestern Europe, between France and Spain. Capital, Andorra la Vella. (p. 43)

Angola (ang gō′ lə) A country on the west coast of southern Africa. Capital, Luanda. (p. 57)

Ankara (ang′ kər ə) The capital of Turkey; 39°N, 32°E. (p. 51)

Annapolis (ə nap′ ə lis) The capital of Maryland; 39°N, 76°W. (p. 15)

Antananarivo (än tə nä nə rē′ vō) The capital of Madagascar; 18°S, 47°E. (p. 57)

Antarctica (ant ärk′ ti kə) The fifth-largest continent. Ice-covered, it surrounds the South Pole and lies mainly within the Antarctic Circle. (p. 2)

Antarctic Ocean (ant ärk′ tik ō′ shən) A body of water surrounding Antarctica, consisting of the southernmost parts of the Atlantic, Pacific, and Indian oceans. (p. 71)

Antigua and Barbuda (an tē′ gə and bär bü′ də) An island nation of the West Indies. Capital, St. John's. (p. 35)

Apennines (ap′ ə nīnz) A mountain range located in central Italy. (p. 42)

Apia (ä pē′ ə) The capital of Western Samoa; 14°S, 172°W. (p. 71)

Appalachian Mountains (ap ə lā′ chē ən moun′ tənz) Low, rounded mountains that cover much of the eastern United States from Maine to Alabama. (p. 14)

Arabian Peninsula (ə rā′ bē ən pə nin′ sə lə) A large peninsula in southwestern Asia. (p. 50)

Arabian Sea (ə rā′ bē ən sē) The northwestern part of the Indian Ocean. (p. 50)

Arafura Sea (ar ə für′ ə sē) A body of water between northern Australia and Indonesia. (p. 70)

Aral Sea (ar′ əl sē) A saltwater lake in the southwestern part of central Asia. (p. 42)

Arctic Ocean (ärk′ tik ō′ shən) The world's smallest ocean. It surrounds the North Pole. (p. 2)

Argentina (är jən tē′ nə) The second-largest country in South America. Capital, Buenos Aires. (p. 35)

Arizona (ar ə zō′ nə) A state in the southwestern United States, bordering Mexico. Capital, Phoenix. (p. 15)

Arkansas (är′ kən sô) A state in the southeastern United States. Capital, Little Rock. (p. 15)

Armenia (är mē′ nē ə) A country in eastern Europe, formerly part of the Soviet Union. Capital, Yerevan. (p. 43)

Aruba (ə rü′ bə) An island in the Caribbean Sea, part of the Netherlands Antilles. (p. 35)

Ashkhabad (ash′ kə bäd) The capital of Turkmenistan; 38°N, 57°E. (p. 43)

Asia (ā′ zhə) The world's largest continent, bounded on the west by Europe, on the east by the Pacific Ocean, and on the south by the Indian Ocean. (p. 3)

Asia Minor (ā′ zhə mī′ nər) A peninsula in western Asia, bordered by the Mediterranean and Black seas. It is also known as Anatolia. (p. 50)

Asunción (ä sün syōn′) The capital and largest city of Paraguay; 25°S, 57°W. (p. 35)

Athens (ath′ ənz) The capital of Greece; 38°N, 24°E. (p. 15)

Atlanta (at lan′ tə) The capital and largest city of Georgia; 33°N, 84°W. (p. 15)

Atlantic Ocean (at lan′ tik ō′ shən) The world's second-largest ocean. It separates North America and South America from Europe and Africa. (p. 2)

Atlas Mountains (at′ ləs moun′ tənz) A mountain range extending along the northwestern coast of Africa. (p. 50)

Augusta (ô gus′ tə) The capital of Maine; 44°N, 69°W. (p. 15)

Austin (ôs′ tin) The capital of Texas; 30°N, 97°W. (p. 15)

Australia (ôs trāl′ yə) The world's smallest continent. Also, a country including the continent of Australia and the island of Tasmania. Capital, Canberra. (p. 71)

Austria (ôs′ trē ə) A country in central Europe. Capital, Vienna. (p. 43)

Azerbaijan (ä zər bī jän′) A country in the Caucasus Mountain region of eastern Europe, formerly part of the Soviet Union. Capital, Baku. (p. 43)

Azores (ə zôrz′) An island group in the northern Atlantic Ocean, west of and belonging to Portugal. (p. 4)

B

Baffin Bay (baf′ in bā) An inlet of the Atlantic Ocean, between Greenland and Baffin Island. (p. 14)

Baghdad (bag′ dad) The capital of Iraq; 33°N, 44°E. (p. 51)

Bahamas (bə hä′ məz) An island country in the West Indies. Capital, Nassau. (p. 35)

Bahrain (bä rān′) An Arab emirate consisting of more than 30 islands in the Persian Gulf. Capital, Manama. (p. 51)

Baku (bä kü′) The capital of Azerbaijan; 40°N, 50°E. (p. 43)

Balearic Islands (bal ē ar′ ik ī′ ləndz) A Spanish island group in the western Mediterranean Sea. (p. 43)

Balkan Peninsula (bôl′ kən pə nin′ sə lə) A large peninsula in southern Europe bounded by the Black, Aegean, and Adriatic seas. (p. 42)

Baltic Sea (bôl′ tik sē) An inland sea in northern Europe. (p. 42)

Bamako (bä mə kō′) The capital of Mali; 12°N, 8°W. (p. 57)

Bandar Seri Begawan (bun′ dər ser′ ē bə gä′ wən) The capital of Brunei; 6°N, 115°E. (p. 65)

Bangkok (bang′ kok) The capital and largest city of Thailand; 13°N, 100°E. (p. 65)

Bangladesh (bang glə desh′) A country located at the northern end of the Bay of Bengal and largely surrounded by India. Capital, Dhaka. (p. 65)

Bangui (bäng′ gē) The capital of the Central African Republic; 5°N, 18°E. (p. 57)

Banjul (bän′ jul) The capital of Gambia; 13°N, 16°W. (p. 57)

Barbados (bär bā′ dōs) An island nation in the Caribbean Sea, the easternmost island of the West Indies. Capital, Bridgetown. (p. 35)

Barents Sea (bar′ ənts sē) An arm of the Arctic Ocean north of Norway and Russia. (p. 42)

Basseterre (bäs târ′) The capital and largest city of St. Kitts and Nevis; 17°N, 62°W. (p. 35)

Baton Rouge (bat′ ən rüzh) The capital of Louisiana; 30°N, 91°W. (p. 15)

Bay of Bengal (bā əv ben′ gôl) The northeastern part of the Indian Ocean. (p. 64)

Bay of Biscay (bā əv bis′ kā) A broad inlet of the northern Atlantic Ocean, between western France and northern Spain. (p. 42)

Beaufort Sea (bō′ fərt sē) An arm of the Arctic, bordering northern Alaska and northwestern Canada. (p. 14)

Beijing (bā′ jing′) The capital of the People's Republic of China. It is also called Peking; 40°N, 116°E. (p. 65)

Beirut (bā rüt′) The capital and largest city of Lebanon; 33°N, 35°E. (p. 51)

Belarus (be lä rüs′) A country in eastern Europe, formerly part of the Soviet Union. Capital, Minsk. (p. 43)

Belfast (bel′ fast) The capital and largest city of Northern Ireland; 54°N, 5°W. (p. 43)

Belgium (bel′ jəm) A country in northwestern Europe, on the North Sea. Capital, Brussels. (p. 43)

Belgrade (bel′ grād) The capital and largest city of Yugoslavia; 44°N, 20°E. (p. 43)

Belize (be lēz′) A country on the northeastern coast of Central America. Capital, Belmopan. (p. 35)

Belmopan (bel mō pän′) The capital of Belize; 17°N, 89°W. (p. 35)

Benin (be nēn′) A country in western Africa, on the Gulf of Guinea. Capital, Porto-Novo. (p. 57)

Bering Sea (ber′ ing sē) The northernmost arm of the Pacific Ocean, between Siberia and Alaska. (p. 14)

Bering Strait (ber′ ing strāt) A strait connecting the Bering Sea with the Arctic Ocean. (p. 14)

Bermuda (bər mū′ də) A British island group in the northern Atlantic Ocean. (p. 4)

Bern (bûrn) The capital of Switzerland; 46°N, 7°E. (p. 43)

Bhutan (bü tän′) A country in south-central Asia, in the Himalayas. Capital, Thimphu. (p. 65)

Bishkek (bish′ kek) The capital of Kyrgyzstan; 43°N, 75°E. (p. 43)

Bismarck (biz′ märk) The capital of North Dakota; 46°N, 100°W. (p. 15)

Bissau (bi sou′) The capital of Guinea-Bissau; 11°N, 15°W. (p. 57)

Black Sea (blak sē) An inland sea between Europe and Asia. (p. 42)

Bloemfontein (blüm′ fən tān) The judicial capital of the Republic of South Africa; 29°S, 26°E. (p. 57)

Blue Ridge Mountains (blü rij moun′ tənz) An eastern range of the Appalachian Mountains. (p. 24)

Bogotá (bō′ gə tä) The capital and largest city of Colombia; 5°N, 73°W. (p. 35)

Boise (boi′ zē) The capital of Idaho; 43°N, 116°W. (p. 15)

Bolivia (bə liv′ ē ə) A country in west-central South America. Capitals, La Paz and Sucre. (p. 35)

Bosnia and Herzegovina (boz′ nē ə and hûrt sə gō vē′ nə) A country in southeastern Europe, formerly part of Yugoslavia. Capital, Sarajevo. (p. 43)

Bosporus (bos′ pər əs) A strait connecting the Black Sea and the Sea of Marmara. (p. 42)

Boston (bôs′ tən) The capital of Massachusetts; 42°N, 71°W. (p. 15)

Botswana (bot swä′ nə) A country in south-central Africa. Capital, Gaborone. (p. 57)

Brahmaputra River (brä mə pü′ trə riv′ ər) A major river of southern Asia, flowing south from Tibet into the Bay of Bengal. Length, 1,770 miles (2,848 km). (p. 64)

Brasília (brə zēl′ yə) The capital of Brazil; 16°S, 48°W. (p. 35)

Brazil (brə zil′) The largest country in South America, on the Atlantic Ocean in the northeastern part of the continent. Capital, Brasília. (p. 35)

Brazzaville (bräz′ ə vēl) The capital of Congo; 4°S, 15°E. (p. 57)

Bridgetown (brij′ toun) The capital of Barbados; 14°N, 59°W. (p. 35)

British Isles (brit′ ish īlz) A group of islands off the western coast of Europe, made up of Britain, Ireland, and many smaller islands. (p. 42)

Brunei (brü nī′) A country on the northern coast of Borneo in southeastern Asia. Capital, Bandar Seri Begawan. (p. 65)

Brussels (brus′ əlz) The capital of Belgium; 51°N, 5°E. (p. 43)

Bucharest (bü′ kə rest) The capital and largest city of Romania; 44°N, 26°E. (p. 43)

Budapest (bü′ də pest) The capital and largest city of Hungary; 47°N, 19°E. (p. 43)

Buenos Aires (bwā′ nəs ī′ rəs) The capital of Argentina; 34°S, 58°W. (p. 35)

Bujumbura (bü jəm bûr′ ə) The capital of Burundi; 4°S, 31°E. (p. 57)

Bulgaria (bul gâr′ ē ə) A country in southeastern Europe. Capital, Sofia. (p. 43)

Burkina Faso (bər kē′ nə fä′ sō) A country in western Africa. Capital, Ouagadougou. (p. 57)

Burundi (bə run′ dē) A country in central Africa. Capital, Bujumbura. (p. 57)

C

Cairo (kī′ rō) The capital of Egypt; 30°N, 31°E. (p. 51)

California (kal ə fôr′ nyə) The most populated state of the United States, on the Pacific. Capital, Sacramento. (p. 15)

Cambodia (kam bō′ dē ə) A country in southeastern Asia, also known as Kampuchea. Capital, Phnom Penh. (p. 65)

Cameroon (kam ə rün′) A country in west-central Africa. Capital, Yaoundé. (p. 57)

Canada (kan′ ə də) A country in northern North America, bordering on the United States. Capital, Ottawa. (p. 15)

Canadian Shield (kə nā′ dē ən shēld) The plains and hills that surround Hudson Bay and cover about half of Canada. (p. 14)

Canary Islands (kə nâr′ ē ī′ ləndz) A Spanish island group in the northern Atlantic Ocean, off the northwestern coast of Africa. (p. 5)

Canberra (kan′ ber ə) The capital of Australia; 35°S, 149°E. (p. 71)

Cape Horn (kāp hôrn) A cape on an island of Tierra del Fuego, forming the southernmost tip of South America; 57°S, 64°W. (p. 34)

Cape of Good Hope (kāp əv gùd hōp) A cape at the southernmost tip of Africa, on the Atlantic Ocean; 34°S, 19°E. (p. 56)

Cape Town (kāp′ toun) The legislative capital of the Republic of South Africa; 34°S, 18°E. (p. 57)

Cape Verde (kāp vûrd) An island country in the northern Atlantic Ocean. Capital, Praia. (p. 4)

Caracas (kə rä′ kəs) The capital and largest city of Venezuela; 10°N, 66°W. (p. 35)

Caribbean Sea (kar ə bē′ ən sē) A sea bounded on the north and east by the West Indies, on the west by Central America, and on the south by South America. (p. 4)

Carpathian Mountains (kär pā′ thē ən moun′ tənz) A mountain system of eastern Europe extending southward toward the Black Sea. (p. 42)

Carson City (kär′ sən sit′ ē) The capital of Nevada; 39°N, 119°W. (p. 15)

Cascade Range (kas kād′ rānj) A mountain range in the western United States, extending from northern California through Oregon and into Washington. (p. 14)

Caspian Sea (kas′ pē ən sē) The largest inland body of water in the world, located in south-central Asia. (p. 42)

Castries (kas trēz′) The capital and largest city of St. Lucia; 14°N, 61°W. (p. 35)

Caucasus Mountains (kô′ kə səs moun′ tənz) A mountain range forming part of the boundary between Europe and Asia. (p. 42)

Cayenne (kī en′) The capital of French Guiana; 4°N, 52°W. (p. 35)

Celebes Sea (sel′ ə bēz sē) An arm of the Pacific Ocean, lying between the Philippines and Indonesia. (p. 64)

Central African Republic (sen′ trəl af′ ri kən ri pub′ lik) A country in central Africa. Capital, Bangui. (p. 57)

Central Valley (sen′ trəl val′ ē) A valley in central California. (p. 30)

Chad (chad) A country in north-central Africa. Capital, Ndjamena. (p. 57)

Chang River (chäng riv′ ər) The longest river in China. It is also known as the Chang Jiang and the Yangtze River. Length, 3,964 miles (6,342 km). (p. 64)

Charleston (chärlz′ tən) The capital of West Virginia; 38°N, 81°W. (p. 15)

Cherskiy Mountains (cher′ skē moun′ tənz) A mountain range in the northeastern part of Russia. (p. 42)

Chesapeake Bay (ches′ ə pēk bā) A bay of the Atlantic Ocean, partly surrounded by Virginia and Maryland. (p. 22)

Cheyenne (shī en′) The capital and largest city of Wyoming; 41°N, 104°W. (p. 15)

Chile (chil′ ē) A country on the southwestern coast of South America. Capital, Santiago. (p. 35)

China, People's Republic of (chī′ nə, pē′ pəlz ri pub′ lik əv) A country in eastern Asia. Capital, Beijing. (p. 65)

Coastal Plains (kōs′ təl plānz) The lowland plains of the United States lying along the Atlantic Ocean and the Gulf of Mexico. (p. 24)

Colombia (kə lum′ bē ə) A country in northwestern South America, on the Pacific Ocean and the Caribbean Sea. Capital, Bogotá. (p. 35)

Colombo (kə lum′ bō) The capital and chief port of Sri Lanka; 6°N, 79°E. (p. 65)

Colorado (kol ə rad′ ō) A state in the western United States. Capital, Denver. (p. 15)

Colorado River (kol ə rad′ ō riv′ ər) A river flowing from northern Colorado into the Gulf of California. Length, 1,450 miles (2,333 km). (p. 14)

Columbia (kə lum′ bē ə) The capital of South Carolina; 34°N, 81°W. (p. 15)

Columbus (kə lum′ bəs) The capital of Ohio; 40°N, 83°W. (p. 15)

Comoros (kom′ ə rōz) An island country off the southeastern coast of Africa. Capital, Moroni. (p. 57)

Conakry (kon′ ə krē) The capital of Guinea; 9°N, 13°W. (p. 57)

Concord (kon′ kôrd) The capital of New Hampshire; 43°N, 71°W. (p. 15)

Congo (kong′ go) A country in east-central Africa. Capital, Brazzaville. (p. 57)

Congo River (kong′ gō) The seventh-largest river in the world, located in central Africa. Length, 2,900 miles (4,640 km). (p. 11)

Connecticut (kə net′ i kət) A state in the northeastern United States. Capital, Hartford. (p. 15)

Connecticut River (kə net′ i kət riv′ ər) The longest river in New England, flowing from northern New Hampshire into Long Island Sound. Length, 407 miles (655 km). (p. 22)

Cook Islands (kùk ī′ ləndz) A group of islands east of Australia in the western part of the southern Pacific Ocean, a possession of New Zealand. (p. 71)

Copenhagen (kō′ pən hā gən) The capital and largest city of Denmark; 56°N, 12°E. (p. 43)

Coral Sea (kôr′ əl sē) A southwestern arm of the Pacific Ocean, off the coast of northeastern Australia. (p. 70)

Corsica (kôr′ si kə) A French island in the Mediterranean Sea, southeast of France. (p. 43)

Costa Rica (kos′ tə rē′ kə) A country in Central America, between Nicaragua and Panama. Capital, San José. (p. 35)

Côte d'Ivoire (kōt dē vwär′) A country in western Africa, formerly known as the Ivory Coast. Capital, Yamoussoukro. (p. 57)

---

a cap; ā cake; ä father; är car; âr dare; ch chain; e hen; ē me; êr clear; hw where; i bib; ī kite; ng song; o top; ō rope; ô saw; oi coin; ôr fork; ou cow; sh show; th thin; th those; u sun; ù book; ü moon; ū cute; ûr term; ə about, taken, pencil, apron, helpful; ər letter, dollar, doctor

Crete (krēt) A Greek island in the Mediterranean Sea, southeast of mainland Greece. (p. 43)

Croatia (krō ā′ shə) A country in southeastern Europe, formerly part of Yugoslavia. Capital, Zagreb. (p. 43)

Cuba (kū′ bə) An island country in the Caribbean Sea, the largest and westernmost island of the West Indies. Capital, Havana. (p. 35)

Cyprus (sī′ prəs) An island country south of Turkey in the eastern Mediterranean Sea. Capital, Nicosia. (p. 51)

Czech Republic (chek re pub′ lik) A country in central Europe. Capital, Prague. (p. 43)

D

Dakar (dä kär′) The capital and largest city of Senegal; 14°N, 17°W. (p. 57)

Damascus (də mas′ kəs) The capital and largest city of Syria; 33°N, 36°E. (p. 51)

Danube River (dan′ ūb riv′ ər) The second-longest river in Europe, flowing eastward from the southern part of Germany into the Black Sea. Length, 1,776 miles (2,858 km). (p. 42)

Dar es Salaam (där es sə läm′) The capital and largest city of Tanzania; 6°S, 39°E. (p. 57)

Darling River (där′ ling riv′ ər) A river in Australia, flowing southwest through western New South Wales to the Murray River. (p. 70)

Dead Sea (ded sē) A salt lake between Israel on the west and Jordan on the east. (p. 50)

Death Valley (deth val′ ē) A deep desert basin in southeastern California. It is the hottest and driest place in the United States and contains the lowest point in the Western Hemisphere. (p. 30)

Delaware (del′ ə wâr) A state in the eastern United States. Capital, Dover. (p. 15)

Delaware Bay (del′ ə wâr bā) An inlet of the Atlantic Ocean between Delaware and New Jersey. (p. 22)

Denmark (den′ märk) A country in northern Europe, between the North and Baltic seas. Capital, Copenhagen. (p. 43)

Denver (den′ vər) The capital of Colorado; 40°N, 103°W. (p. 15)

Des Moines (də moin′) The capital and largest city of Iowa; 41°N, 91°W. (p. 15)

Dhaka (dak′ ə) The capital and largest city of Bangladesh; 25°N, 91°E. (p. 65)

Djibouti (ji bü′ tē) A country in east Africa, on the Gulf of Aden. Capital, Djibouti. (p. 57)

Djibouti (ji bü′ tē) The capital of Djibouti; 11°N, 43°E. (p. 57)

Dnieper River (nē′ pər riv′ ər) A river flowing through eastern Europe into the Black Sea. Length, 1,368 miles (2,201 km). (p. 42)

Dniester River (nēs′ tər riv′ ər) A river flowing through Ukraine and Moldova into the Black Sea. Length, 840 miles (1,352 km). (p. 42)

Dodoma (dō′ də mə) A capital of Tanzania; 6°S, 35°E. (p. 57)

Doha (dō′ hä) The capital of Qatar; 25°N, 52°E. (p. 51)

Dominica (dom ə nē′ kə) A country in the eastern West Indies, one of the Windward Islands. Capital, Roseau. (p. 35)

Dominican Republic (də min′ i kən ri pub′ lik) A country in the central West Indies, occupying the eastern part of the island of Hispaniola. Capital, Santo Domingo. (p. 35)

Don River (don riv′ ər) A river flowing through Russia into the Sea of Azov. Length, 1,224 miles (1,969 km). (p. 42)

Dover (dō′ vər) The capital of Delaware; 39°N, 75°W. (p. 15)

Drakensberg Mountains (drä′ kənz bûrg moun′ tənz) A mountain range in southeastern Africa. (p. 56)

Dublin (dub′ lin) The capital and largest city of the Republic of Ireland; 53°N, 6°W. (p. 43)

Dushanbe (dyü shan′ bə) The capital of Tajikistan; 38°N, 69°E. (p. 43)

E

East China Sea (ēst chī′ nə sē) An arm of the Pacific Ocean between eastern China and the Ryukyu Islands. (p. 65)

Ecuador (ek′ wə dôr) A country on the northwestern coast of South America. Capital, Quito. (p. 35)

Edinburgh (ed′ ən bûr ō) The capital of Scotland; 55°N, 3°W. (p. 43)

Egypt (ē′ jipt) A country in northeastern Africa. Capital, Cairo. (p. 51)

El Aaiún (el ä ün′) The capital of Western Sahara; 27°N, 13°W. (p. 51)

Elbe River (el′ bə riv′ ər) A river in central Europe, flowing from the Czech Republic into the North Sea. Length, 720 miles (1,158 km). (p. 42)

Elburz Mountains (el bürz′ moun′ tənz) A mountain range in northern Iran. (p. 50)

Ellesmere Island (elz′ mîr ī′ lənd) A large Canadian island in the Arctic Ocean, northwest of Greenland. (p. 15)

El Salvador (el sal′ və dôr) A country in western Central America. Capital, San Salvador. (p. 35)

English Channel (ing′ glish chan′ əl) A narrow body of water between Great Britain and northwestern Europe. (p. 42)

Equatorial Guinea (ē kwə tôr′ ē əl gin′ ē) A country in west-central Africa. Capital, Malabo. (p. 57)

Estonia (es tō′ nē ə) A country on the Baltic Sea, formerly part of the Soviet Union. Capital, Tallinn. (p. 43)

Ethiopia (ē thē ō′ pē ə) A country in eastern Africa. Capital, Addis Ababa. (p. 57)

Euphrates River (ū frā′ tēz riv′ ər) A river in the Middle East flowing from Turkey into the Persian Gulf. Length, 1,510 miles (2,430 km). (p. 50)

Europe (yür′ əp) The world's sixth-largest continent. It lies between the Atlantic Ocean and Asia, from which it is separated by the Ural and Caucasus mountains. (p. 3)

F

Falkland Islands (fôk′ lənd ī′ ləndz) An island group in the southern Atlantic Ocean. A British dependency, they are also claimed by Argentina. (p. 34)

Federated States of Micronesia (fed′ ər ā ted stāts əv mī krō nē′ zhə) A country in the Pacific Ocean made up of a group of islands. Capital, Kolonia. (p. 71)

Fiji (fē′ jē) A country consisting of some 800 islands north of New Zealand, in the southwestern Pacific Ocean. Capital, Suva. (p. 71)

Finland (fin′ lənd) A nation in northeastern Europe, on the Baltic Sea. Capital, Helsinki. (p. 43)

Florida (flôr′ i də) A state mostly on the southeastern peninsula of the United States. Capital, Tallahassee. (p. 15)

France (frans) A country in western Europe. Capital, Paris. (p. 43)

Frankfort (frangk′ fərt) The capital of Kentucky; 38°N, 84°W. (p. 15)

Freetown (frē′ toun) The capital of Sierra Leone; 8°N, 13°W. (p. 57)

French Guiana (french gē an′ ə) An overseas department of France, on the northeastern coast of South America. Capital, Cayenne. (p. 35)

French Polynesia (french pol ə nē′ zhə) A French possession in the southeastern Pacific Ocean consisting of several islands, including Tahiti. (p. 71)

Funafuti (fü nə fü′ tē) The capital of Tuvalu; 6°S, 166°E. (p. 71)

G

Gabon (ga bōn′) A country on the west coast of central Africa. Capital, Libreville. (p. 57)

Gaborone (gä bə rō′ nē) The capital of Botswana; 24°S, 25°E. (p. 57)

Gambia, (The) (gam′ bē ə) A country on the western coast of Africa. Capital, Banjul. (p. 57)

Gambia River (gam′ bē ə riv′ ər) A river in west Africa, flowing through Senegal and into the Atlantic Ocean. Length, 200 miles (322 km). (p. 56)

Ganges River (gan′ jēz riv′ ər) A river in northern India and Bangladesh, flowing from the Himalayas into the Bay of Bengal. Length, 1,560 miles (2,510 km). (p. 64)

Georgetown (jôrg′ toun) The capital and largest city of Guyana; 7°N, 58°W. (p. 35)

Georgia (jôr′ jə) A country in the Caucasus Mountain region, formerly part of the Soviet Union. Capital, Tbilisi. (p. 43)

Georgia (jôr′ jə) A state in the southeastern United States. Capital, Atlanta. (p. 15)

Germany (jûr′ mə nē) A country in north-central Europe. Capital, Berlin. (p. 43)

Ghana (gä′ nə) A country in western Africa, on the Gulf of Guinea. Capital, Accra. (p. 57)

Gibraltar (ji brôl′ tər) A British crown colony and seaport near the southern tip of Spain. (p. 43)

Gobi (gō′ bē) A large desert in southeastern Mongolia and northern China. (p. 64)

Gran Chaco (grän chä′ kō) A vast lowland region in south-central South America. (p. 34)

Grand Canyon (grand can′ yən) A large canyon in northwestern Arizona on the Colorado River; 36°N, 112°W. (p. 38)

Great Barrier Reef (grāt bar′ ē ər rēf) The largest barrier reef in the world, lying off the northeastern coast of Australia. (p. 70)

Great Basin (grāt bā′ sin) A low, bowl-shaped desert area located in the western part of the United States. (p. 30)

Great Britain (grāt brit′ ən) An island off the western coast of Europe that includes England, Scotland, and Wales. (p. 43)

Great Dividing Range (grāt di vīd′ ing rānj) Highlands extending along the eastern coast of Australia. (p. 70)

Greater Antilles (grāt′ ər an til′ ēz) An island group of the West Indies, including Cuba, Jamaica, Hispaniola, and Puerto Rico. (p. 34)

Great Lakes (grāt lāks) Five freshwater lakes lying along the border between Canada and the United States. They are Lake Superior, Lake Huron, Lake Michigan, Lake Erie, and Lake Ontario. (p. 14)

Great Plains (grāt plānz) The western, nearly treeless part of the Interior Plains of North America. (p. 14)

Great Salt Lake (grāt sôlt lāk) A lake in northwestern Utah, the largest salt lake in North America. (p. 14)

Great Slave Lake (grāt slāv lāk) A lake in the southwestern part of the Northwest Territories, Canada. (p. 14)

Greece (grēs) A country at the southern end of the Balkan Peninsula. Capital, Athens. (p. 43)

Greenland (grēn′ lənd) The largest island in the world, lying mostly within the Arctic Circle. (p. 14)

Grenada (gri nā′ də) An island country in the West Indies, one of the Windward Islands. Capital, St. George's. (p. 35)

Grenadines (gren′ ə dēnz) An island group in the Windward Islands, divided politically into Grenada and St. Vincent and the Grenadines. (p. 35)

Guadeloupe (gwä də lüp′) A French department in the West Indies, consisting of two islands in the Leeward Islands. (p. 35)

Guam (gwäm) An island in the western Pacific Ocean, east of the Philippines. It is a territory of the United States. Capital, Agana. (p. 5)

Guatemala (gwä tə mä′ lə) The northernmost country of Central America. Capital, Guatemala City. (p. 35)

Guatemala City (gwä tə mä′ lə sit′ ē) The capital and largest city of Guatemala; 14°N, 90°W. (p. 35)

Guinea (gin′ ē) A country on the Atlantic Ocean in western Africa. Capital, Conakry. (p. 57)

---

a cap; ā cake; ä father; är car; âr dare; ch chain; e hen; ē me; êr clear; hw where; i bib; ī kite; ng song; o top; ō rope; ô saw; oi coin; ôr fork; ou cow; sh show; th thin; <u>th</u> those; u sun; ù book; ü moon; ū cute; ûr term; ə about, taken, pencil, apron, helpful; ər letter, dollar, doctor

Guinea-Bissau (gin′ ē bē sou′) A country on the Atlantic Ocean in western Africa. Capital, Bissau. (p. 57)

Gulf of Aden (gulf əv ā′ dən) A western inlet of the Arabian Sea. (p. 50)

Gulf of Bothnia (gulf əv both′ nē ə) The northern arm of the Baltic Sea, between Sweden and Finland. (p. 43)

Gulf of California (gulf əv kal ə fôr′ nyə) A long inlet of the Pacific Ocean, just south of California. (p. 34)

Gulf of Mexico (gulf əv mek′ si kō) An arm of the Atlantic Ocean, between the United States and Mexico. (p. 34)

Gulf of Oman (gulf əv ō män′) A northern inlet of the Arabian Sea. (p. 50)

Gulf of St. Lawrence (gulf əv sānt lôr′ əns) An arm of the Atlantic Ocean, on the eastern coast of Canada, at the mouth of the St. Lawrence River. (p. 14)

Gulf of Tonkin (gulf əv ton′ kin′) An arm of the South China Sea, bordered by Vietnam and China. (p. 64)

Guyana (gī an′ ə) A country on the northeastern coast of South America. Capital, Georgetown. (p. 35)

H

Haiti (hā′ tē) A country in the Caribbean Sea, on the western part of the island of Hispaniola. Capital, Port-au-Prince. (p. 35)

Hanoi (ha noi′) The capital of Vietnam; 21°N, 105°E. (p. 65)

Harare (hə rär′ ā) The capital and largest city of Zimbabwe; 18°S, 13°E. (p. 57)

Harrisburg (har′ is bûrg) The capital of Pennsylvania; 40°N, 76°W. (p. 15)

Hartford (härt′ fərd) The capital of Connecticut; 41°N, 72°W. (p. 15)

Havana (hə van′ ə) The capital of Cuba; 23°N, 82°W. (p. 35)

Hawaii (hə wī′ ē) A state of the United States, made up of the Hawaiian Islands. It is the only island state of the United States and the only state not on the North American continent. Capital, Honolulu. (p. 15)

Helena (hel′ ə nə) The capital of Montana; 46°N, 112°W. (p. 15)

Helsinki (hel sing′ kē) The capital and largest city of Finland; 60°N, 24°E. (p. 43)

Himalayas (him ə lā′ əz) The highest mountain system in the world, forming part of the northern boundary of the Indian subcontinent. (p. 64)

Hindu Kush (hin′ dü kush′) A mountain system of central Asia, largely in northeastern Afghanistan. (p. 64)

Hispaniola (his pən yō′ lə) An island in the Caribbean Sea, divided into the Dominican Republic and Haiti. (p. 34)

Honduras (hon dùr′ əs) A country in northern Central America. Capital, Tegucigalpa. (p. 35)

Hong Kong (hong kong) A British crown colony off the southeastern coast of China. It will return to Chinese control after 1997; 22°N, 115°E. (p. 65)

Honiara (hō nē är′ ə) The capital of the Solomon Islands; 10°S, 146°E. (p. 71)

Honolulu (hon ə lü′ lü) The capital and largest city of Hawaii; 21°N, 157°W. (p. 15)

Huang River (hwäng riv′ ər) A large river that flows across China into the Yellow Sea. It is also known as the Huang Ho and the Yellow River. Length, 2,903 miles (4,644 km). (p. 64)

Hudson Bay (hud′ sən bā) A large inland sea in northeastern Canada. (p. 14)

Hudson River (hud′ sən riv′ ər) A river in eastern New York, flowing south into New York Bay. Length, 306 miles (492 km). (p. 22)

Hungary (hung′ gə rē) A country in east-central Europe. Capital, Budapest. (p. 43)

I

Iberian Peninsula (ī bîr′ ē ən pə nin′ sə lə) A large peninsula in southwestern Europe, between the Atlantic Ocean and the Mediterranean Sea. (p. 42)

Iceland (īs′ lənd) An island country in the northern Atlantic Ocean, between Greenland and Norway. Capital, Reykjavik. (p. 43)

Idaho (ī′ də hō) A state in the western United States. Capital, Boise. (p. 15)

Illinois (il ə noi′) A state in the north-central United States. Capital, Springfield. (p. 15)

India (in′ dē ə) A country in southern Asia. Capital, New Delhi. (p. 65)

Indiana (in dē an′ ə) A state in the north-central United States. Capital, Indianapolis. (p. 15)

Indianapolis (in dē ə nap′ ə lis) The capital and largest city of Indiana; 39°N, 86°W. (p. 15)

Indian Ocean (in′ dē ən ō′ shən) An ocean south of Asia, between Africa and Australia. (p. 3)

Indonesia (in də nē′ zhə) A country in southeastern Asia composed of thousands of islands. Capital, Jakarta. (p. 65)

Indus River (in′ dəs riv′ ər) A river flowing from Tibet through Kashmir and Pakistan into the Arabian Sea. Length, 1,800 miles (2,896 km). (p. 64)

Inner Mongolia (in′ ər môn gō′ lē ə) An autonomous region of China, in the northern part of the country. (p. 64)

Interior Plains (in tîr′ ē ər plānz) Plains covering much of the central part of North America. (p. 14)

Iowa (ī′ ə wə) A state in the north-central United States. Capital, Des Moines. (p. 15)

Iran (i ran′) A country in southwestern Asia. Capital, Tehran. (p. 51)

Iraq (i rak′) A country in southwestern Asia. Capital, Baghdad. (p. 51)

Ireland, Republic of (īr′ lənd, re pub′ lik əv) A country in northwestern Europe, on the island of Ireland. Capital, Dublin. (p. 43)

Irrawaddy River (ēr′ ə wod′ ē riv′ ər) A river flowing through Myanmar (Burma) into the Bay of Bengal. Length, 1,000 miles (1,600 km). (p. 64)

Irtysh River (îr tish′ riv′ ər) A river of central Asia, flowing northwest and north from the Altai Mountains in China into the Ob River in Siberia. Length, 2,747 miles (4,420 km). (p. 42)

Islamabad (is lä′ mə bäd) The capital of Pakistan; 33°N, 73°E. (p. 65)

Israel (iz′ rā əl) A country in southwestern Asia at the eastern end of the Mediterranean Sea. Capital, Jerusalem. (p. 51)

Isthmus of Panama (is′ məs əv pan′ ə mä) A narrow strip of land connecting North America and South America. (p. 34)

Italian Peninsula (i tal′ yən pə nin′ sə lə) A long peninsula in Southern Europe on which Italy is located. (p. 42)

Italy (it′ ə lē) A country in southern Europe, on the Mediterranean Sea. Capital, Rome. (p. 43)

J

Jackson (jak′ sən) The capital of Mississippi; 32°N, 90°W. (p. 15)

Jakarta (jə kär′ tə) The capital and largest city of Indonesia; 6°S, 107°E. (p. 65)

Jamaica (jə mā′ kə) An island country in the Caribbean Sea, south of Cuba. Capital, Kingston. (p. 35)

Japan (jə pan′) A country in the northern Pacific Ocean, off the eastern coast of Asia, consisting of a chain of islands. Capital, Tokyo. (p. 65)

Java Sea (jä′ və sē) An arm of the Pacific Ocean, in Indonesia. (p. 64)

Jefferson City (jef′ ər sən sit′ ē) The capital of Missouri; 38°N, 92°W. (p. 15)

Jerusalem (jə rü′ sə ləm) The capital of Israel; 31°N, 35°E. (p. 51)

Jordan (jôr′ dən) A country in southwestern Asia, east of and bordering Israel. Capital, Amman. (p. 51)

Juneau (jü′ nō) The capital of Alaska; 58°N, 136°W. (p. 15)

K

Kabul (kä bül′) The capital of Afghanistan; 33°N, 69°E. (p. 65)

Kalahari Desert (kä lə här′ ē des′ ərt) A large desert in southern Africa. (p. 56)

Kampala (käm pä′ lə) The capital and largest city of Uganda; 1°N, 32°E. (p. 57)

Kansas (kan′ zəs) A state in the west-central United States. Capital, Topeka. (p. 15)

Karakoram Range (kär ə kôr′ əm ränj) A mountain system in central Asia, extending from northern Pakistan and India to southern China. (p. 64)

Kara Sea (kär′ ə sē) An arm of the Arctic Ocean, off the coast of north-central Russia. It is frozen most of the year. (p. 42)

Kathmandu (kat man dü′) The capital of Nepal; 27°N, 85°E. (p. 65)

Kazakhstan (kä zäk stän′) A country in central Asia, formerly part of the Soviet Union. Capital, Alma-Ata. (p. 43)

Kentucky (kən tuk′ ē) A state in the southeast region of the United States. Capital, Frankfort. (p. 15)

Kenya (ken′ yə) A country in eastern Africa. Capital, Nairobi. (p. 57)

Khartoum (kär tüm′) The capital of Sudan; 15°N, 32°E. (p. 57)

Kiev (kē ev′) The capital of Ukraine; 50°N, 30°E. (p. 43)

Kigali (ki gä′ lē) The capital of Rwanda; 1°S, 30°E. (p. 57)

Kingston (kingz′ tən) The capital and largest city of Jamaica; 18°N, 76°W. (p. 35)

Kingstown (kingz′ toun) The capital of St. Vincent and the Grenadines; 13°N, 61°W. (p. 35)

Kinshasa (kin shä′ sə) The capital and largest city of Zaire; 4°S, 15°E. (p. 57)

Kiribati (kîr i bä′ tē) An island nation in the central Pacific Ocean. Capital, Tarawa. (p. 71)

Kishinev (kish′ ə nev) The capital of Moldova; 46°N, 29°E. (p. 43)

Kolonia (kə lō′ nē ə) The capital of the Federated States of Micronesia; 3°N, 160°E. (p. 71)

Korea, North (kə rē ə, nôrth) A country occupying the northern part of the Korean Peninsula. Capital, Pyongyang. (p. 65)

Korea, South (kə rē ə, south) A country occupying the southern part of the Korean Peninsula. Capital, Seoul. (p. 65)

Kuala Lumpur (kwä′ lə lùm púr′) The capital of Malaysia; 3°N, 101°E. (p. 65)

Kuril Islands (kyúr′ əl ī′ ləndz) A group of islands off the coast of Asia, northeast of Japan, east of and belonging to Russia. (p. 42)

Kuwait (kü wāt′) A country in the northeastern part of the peninsula of Arabia. Capital, Kuwait; 29°N, 47°E. (p. 51)

Kyrgyszstan (kêr′ giz stän) A country in central Asia, formerly part of the Soviet Union. Capital, Bishkek. (p. 43)

L

Lake Athabaska (lāk ath ə bas′ kə) A lake in Canada, on the northern Alberta-Saskatchewan border. (p. 14)

Lake Baikal (lāk bī käl′) A lake in southeast-central Russia. It is the deepest freshwater lake in the world. (p. 42)

Lake Chad (lāk chad) A lake in north-central Africa, at the southern edge of the Sahara. (p. 56)

Lake Champlain (lāk sham plān′) A lake on the border between New York and Vermont, extending into southwestern Quebec. (p. 22)

Lake Erie (lāk îr′ ē) The southernmost of the Great Lakes, on the U.S.-Canadian border. (p. 14)

a cap; ā cake; ä father; är car; âr dare; ch chain; e hen; ē me; êr clear; hw where; i bib; ī kite; ng song; o top; ō rope; ô saw; oi coin; ôr fork; ou cow; sh show; th thin; th those; u sun; ù book; ü moon; ū cute; ûr term; ə about, taken, pencil, apron, helpful; ər letter, dollar, doctor

Lake Eyre (lāk âr) A saltwater lake in Australia. (p. 70)

Lake Huron (lāk hyür′ ən) The second largest of the Great Lakes, on the U.S.-Canadian border. (p. 14)

Lake Michigan (lāk mish′ i gən) The third-largest of the Great Lakes. It lies between Michigan and Wisconsin. (p. 14)

Lake Nasser (lāk näs′ ər) A lake in southern Egypt, formed in the 1960s as a result of the construction of the Aswan High Dam. (p. 50)

Lake of the Woods (lāk əv the wüdz) A lake on the border of Minnesota and the Canadian provinces of Manitoba and Ontario. (p. 26)

Lake Ontario (lāk on târ′ ē ō) The smallest and easternmost of the Great Lakes, between New York and Canada. (p. 14)

Lake Superior (lāk sə pîr′ ē ər) The largest and northernmost of the Great Lakes, on the U.S.-Canadian border. (p. 14)

Lake Tanganyika (lāk tan gən yē′ kə) A lake in east-central Africa, lying between Zaire, Tanzania, and Zambia. (p. 56)

Lake Titicaca (lāk tit i kä′ kə) The largest lake in South America and the highest navigable lake in the world. (p. 34)

Lake Victoria (lāk vik tôr′ ē ə) The largest lake in Africa, located in the east-central part of the continent. (p. 57)

Lansing (lan′ sing) The capital of Michigan; 42°N, 84°W. (p. 15)

Laos (lä′ ōs) A country in southeastern Asia, between northern Thailand and northern Vietnam. Capital, Vientiane. (p. 65)

La Paz (lə päz′) The administrative capital of Bolivia; 16°S, 69°W. (p. 35)

Lapland (lap′ land) A region that includes northern Norway, northern Sweden, and northern Finland. (p. 42)

Laptev Sea (lap′ tef sē) An arm of the Arctic Ocean, off the northern coast of Russia. (p. 42)

Latvia (lat′ vē ə) A country on the Baltic Sea, formerly part of the Soviet Union. Capital, Riga. (p. 43)

Lebanon (leb′ ə non) A country in southwestern Asia, on the eastern shore of the Mediterranean Sea. Capital, Beirut. (p. 51)

Lena River (lē′ nə riv′ ər) A river in Russia, flowing through east-central Siberia into the Arctic Ocean. Length, 2,734 miles (4,374 km). (p. 42)

Lesotho (lə sō′ tō) A country in southern Africa, entirely surrounded by the Republic of South Africa. Capital, Maseru. (p. 57)

Lesser Antilles (les′ ər an til′ ēz) The islands, excluding the Bahamas, making up the eastern part of the West Indies, or Caribbean Islands. (p. 34)

Lhasa (lä′ sə) The capital of Tibet; 29°N, 91°E. (p. 65)

Liberia (lī bîr′ ē ə) A country on the west coast of Africa, first settled in 1822 by freed slaves from the United States. Capital, Monrovia. (p. 57)

Libreville (lē′ brə vil) The capital and largest city of Gabon; 1°N, 9°E. (p. 57)

Libya (lib′ ē ə) A country on the coast of northern Africa. Capital, Tripoli. (p. 51)

Liechtenstein (lik′ tən stīn) A country in central Europe, between Austria and Switzerland. Capital, Vaduz. (p. 43)

Lilongwe (li lông′ wā) The capital of Malawi; 13°S, 33°E. (p. 57)

Lima (lē′ mə) The capital of Peru; 12°S, 76°W. (p. 35)

Limpopo River (lim pō′ pō riv′ ər) A river in southeastern Africa, flowing from South Africa through Mozambique into the Indian Ocean. Length, 1,100 miles (1,774 km). (p. 56)

Lincoln (ling′ kən) The capital of Nebraska; 40°N, 96°W. (p. 15)

Lisbon (liz′ bən) The capital and largest city of Portugal; 38°N, 9°W. (p. 43)

Lithuania (lith ü ā′ nē ə) A country on the Baltic Sea, formerly part of the Soviet Union. Capital, Vilnius. (p. 43)

Little Rock (lit′ əl rok) The capital and largest city of Arkansas; 34°N, 92°W. (p. 15)

Ljubljana (lē ü blē än′ ə) The capital of Slovenia; 46°N, 14°E. (p. 43)

Loire River (lwär riv′ ər) The longest river in France, flowing from the south-central part of the country into the Bay of Biscay. Length, 625 miles (1,006 km). (p. 42)

Lomé (lō mā′) The capital of Togo; 6°N, 1°E. (p. 57)

London (lun′ dən) The capital and largest city of the United Kingdom; 51°N, 1°E. (p. 43)

Long Island Sound (lông ī′ lənd sound) An arm of the Atlantic Ocean, separating Connecticut from Long Island, New York. (p. 22)

Louisiana (lü ē zē an′ ə) A state in the southern United States, on the Gulf of Mexico and the Mississippi River. Capital, Baton Rouge. (p. 15)

Luanda (lü an′ də) The capital and largest city of Angola; 8°S, 14°E. (p. 57)

Lusaka (lü sä′ kə) The capital and largest city of Zambia; 15°S, 28°E. (p. 57)

Luxembourg (luk′ səm bûrg) A country in western Europe, bordering France, Belgium, and Germany. Capital, Luxembourg. (p. 43)

Luxembourg (luk′ səm bûrg) The capital and chief city of Luxembourg; 49°N, 6°E. (p. 43)

M

Macedonia (mas ə dō′ nē ə) A country in southeastern Europe, formerly part of Yugoslavia. Capital, Skopje. (p. 43)

Mackenzie River (mə ken′ zē riv′ ər) A river in northwestern Canada. Length, 2,635 miles (4,216 km). (p. 14)

Madagascar (mad ə gas′ kər) An island country in the Indian Ocean. Capital, Antananarivo. (p. 57)

Madison (mad′ ə sən) The capital of Wisconsin; 43°N, 89°W. (p. 15)

Madrid (mə drid′) The capital and largest city of Spain; 40°N, 4°W. (p. 43)

Maine (mān) A state in the northeastern United States. Capital, Augusta. (p. 15)

Majuro (mə jür′ ō) The capital of the Marshall Islands; 8°N, 171°E. (p. 71)

Malabo (mə lä′ bō) The capital of Equatorial Guinea; 3°N, 8°E. (p. 57)

Malawi (mə lä′ wē) A country in southeastern Africa. Capital, Lilongwe. (p. 57)

Malaysia (mə lā′ zhə) A country in southeastern Asia, divided by the South China Sea. Capital, Kuala Lumpur. (p. 65)

Maldives (môl′ dēvz) A country of about 2,000 islands in the Indian Ocean, southwest of India. Capital, Malé. (p. 65)

Malé (mä′ lē) The capital of the Maldives; 5°N, 73°E. (p. 65)

Mali (mä′ lē) A country in western Africa. Capital, Bamako. (p. 57)

Malta (môl′ tə) A country consisting of an island group in the Mediterranean Sea. Capital, Valletta. (p. 43)

Managua (mə nä′ gwə) The capital and largest city of Nicaragua; 12°N, 86°W. (p. 35)

Manama (mə nam′ ə) The capital of Bahrain; 26°N, 50°E. (p. 51)

Manila (mə nil′ ə) The capital and largest city of the Philippines; 14°N, 121°E. (p. 65)

Maputo (mə pü′ tō) The capital of Mozambique; 26°S, 32°E. (p. 57)

Marshall Islands (mär′ shəl ī′ ləndz) An independent group of Pacific islands associated with the United States. Capital, Majuro. (p. 71)

Martinique (mär tə nēk′) A French island in the Caribbean Sea. (p. 35)

Maryland (mer′ ə lənd) A state in the eastern United States. Capital, Annapolis. (p. 15)

Maseru (maz′ ə rü) The capital of Lesotho; 29°S, 27°E. (p. 57)

Massachusetts (mas ə chü′ sits) A state in the northeastern United States. Capital, Boston. (p. 15)

Mauritania (môr i tā′ nē ə) A country on the northwestern coast of Africa. Capital, Nouakchott. (p. 57)

Mauritius (mô rish′ əs) An island country in the western Indian Ocean, east of Madagascar. Capital, Port Louis. (p. 5)

Mayotte (mä yot′) An island in the Indian Ocean. (p. 57)

Mbabane (bä bän′) The capital of Swaziland; 26°S, 31°E. (p. 57)

Mediterranean Sea (med i tə rā′ nē ən sē) A large, nearly landlocked arm of the Atlantic Ocean lying between Europe, Asia, and Africa. (p. 50)

Mekong River (mā′ kong′ riv′ ər) A river in Southeast Asia, flowing from western China southwest into the China Sea. Length, 2,600 miles (4,160 km). (p. 64)

Melanesia (mel ə nē′ zhə) One of the three main divisions of the Pacific islands. (p. 71)

Mesopotamia (mes ə pə tā′ mē ə) A historic region in southwestern Asia, between the Tigris and Euphrates rivers. (p. 50)

Mexico (mek′ si kō) A country in North America, south of and bordering the southwestern United States. Capital, Mexico City. (p. 35)

Mexico City (mek′ si kō sit′ ē) The capital and largest city of Mexico; 19°N, 99°W. (p. 35)

Michigan (mish′ i gən) A state in the north-central United States. Capital, Lansing. (p. 15)

Micronesia (mī krə nē′ zhə) One of the three main divisions of the Pacific islands. (p. 71)

Midway Islands (mid′ wā ī′ ləndz) A small island group in the north-central Pacific Ocean, administered by the United States. (p. 4)

Minnesota (min ə sō′ tə) A state in the north-central United States. Capital, St. Paul. (p. 15)

Minsk (minsk) The capital of Belarus; 53°N, 27°E. (p. 43)

Mississippi (mis ə sip′ ē) A state in the southern United States. Capital, Jackson. (p. 15)

Mississippi River (mis ə sip′ ē riv′ ər) The Mississippi River, when combined with the Missouri River, forms the fourth-longest river system in the world. Length, 3,710 miles (5,936 km). (p. 14)

Missouri (mi zúr′ ē) A state in the central United States. Capital, Jefferson City. (p. 15)

Missouri River (mi zúr′ ē riv′ ər) A large river in the United States, flowing from Montana into the Mississippi River just north of St. Louis. (p. 14)

Mogadishu (mog ə dish′ ü) The capital of Somalia; 2°N, 45°E. (p. 57)

Moldova (môl dō′ və) A country in eastern Europe, formerly part of the Soviet Union. Capital, Kishinev. (p. 43)

Monaco (mon′ ə kō) A country in southern Europe, on the Mediterranean Sea. Capital, Monaco; 43°N, 7°E. (p. 43)

Mongolia (mong gō′ lē ə) A country in central Asia, bordered by Russia and China. Capital, Ulaanbaatar. (p. 65)

Monrovia (mon rō′ vē ə) The capital and largest city of Liberia; 6°N, 10°W. (p. 57)

Montana (mon tan′ ə) A state in the northwestern United States. Capital, Helena. (p. 15)

Montevideo (mon tə vi dā′ ō) The capital of Uruguay; 34°S, 56°W. (p. 35)

Montgomery (mont gum′ ə rē) The capital of Alabama; 32°N, 86°W. (p. 15)

Montpelier (mont pēl′ yər) The capital of Vermont; 44°N, 72°W. (p. 15)

Morocco (mə rok′ ō) A country in northwestern Africa. Capital, Rabat. (p. 51)

Moscow (mos′ kou) The capital and largest city of Russia; 56°N, 38°W. (p. 43)

Mount Aconcagua (mount ak ən kä′ gwə) A mountain peak in the Andes Mountains, the highest in the Western Hemisphere. Height, 22,831 feet (6,959 m); 33°S, 70°W. (p. 34)

Mount Cook (mount kúk) The highest mountain in New Zealand. Height, 12,349 feet (3,764 m); 44°S, 170°E. (p. 70)

---

a cap; ā cake; ä father; är car; âr dare; ch chain; e hen; ē me; êr clear; hw where; i bib; ī kite; ng song; o top; ō rope; ô saw; oi coin; ôr fork; ou cow; sh show; th thin; th those; u sun; ú book; ü moon; ū cute; ûr term; ə about, taken, pencil, apron, helpful; ər letter, dollar, doctor

Mount Elbrus (mount el′ brüs) The highest peak of Europe. Height, 18,481 feet (5,633 m); 43°N, 43°E. (p. 42)

Mount Everest (mount ev′ ər əst) The highest mountain in the world, in the Himalayas. Height, 29,028 feet (8,848 m); 33°N, 87°E. (p. 64)

Mount Kilimanjaro (mount kil ə mən jär′ ō) The highest mountain in Africa, in northeastern Tanzania near the Kenyan border. Height, 19,340 feet (5,895 m); 3°S, 37°E. (p. 56)

Mount Kosciusko (mount kos ē us′ kō) The highest mountain in Australia. Height, 7,310 feet (2,228 m); 37°S, 148°E. (p. 70)

Mount McKinley (mount mə kin′ lē) The highest mountain in North America, in south-central Alaska. Height, 20,320 feet (6,194 m); 62°N, 150°W. (p. 14)

Mount St. Helens (mount sānt hel′ ənz) An active volcano in the state of Washington, in the Cascade Range. Height, 8,364 feet (2,549 m); 53°N, 122°W. (p. 30)

Mozambique (mō zəm bēk′) A country in southeastern Africa. Capital, Maputo. (p. 57)

Murray River (mùr′ ē riv′ ər) The Murray River, when combined with the Darling River, forms the longest river system in Australia. Length, 2,310 miles (3,718 km). (p. 70)

Muscat (mus′ kat) The capital of Oman; 23°N, 58°E. (p. 51)

Myanmar (mē′ ən mär) A country in southeastern Asia, formerly called Burma. Capital, Yangon. (p. 65)

N

Nairobi (nī rō′ bē) The capital of Kenya; 1°S, 36°E. (p. 57)

Namibia (nə mib′ ē ə) A country on the southwestern coast of Africa. Capital, Windhoek. (p. 57)

Nashville (nash′ vil) The capital of Tennessee; 36°N, 86°W. (p. 15)

Nassau (nas′ ô) The capital and largest city of the Bahamas; 25°N, 77°W. (p. 35)

Nauru (nä ü′ rü) An island country in the central Pacific Ocean, northeast of Australia. Capital, Yaren. (p. 71)

N'Djamena (ən jä′ mə nə) The capital of Chad; 3°N, 15°E. (p. 57)

Nebraska (nə bras′ kə) A state in the central United States. Capital, Lincoln. (p. 15)

Nepal (nə pôl′) A country in central Asia, bounded by India and Tibet. Capital, Kathmandu. (p. 65)

Netherlands (neth′ ər ləndz) A country in western Europe, on the North Sea. Capital, Amsterdam; Seat of government, The Hague. (p. 43)

Netherlands Antilles (neth′ ər ləndz an til′ ēz) A Dutch island group in the southern Caribbean Sea. (p. 35)

Nevada (nə vad′ ə) A state in the western United States. Capital, Carson City. (p. 15)

New Caledonia (nü kal i dō′ nē ə) A French island territory in the southern Pacific Ocean, east of Australia. (p. 70)

New Delhi (nü del′ ē) The capital of India; 28°N, 77°E. (p. 65)

New Guinea (nü gin′ ē) The second-largest island in the world, in the western Pacific Ocean, north of Australia. (p. 64)

New Hampshire (nü hamp′ shər) A state in the northeastern United States. Capital, Concord. (p. 15)

New Jersey (nü jûr′ zē) A state in the eastern United States. Capital, Trenton. (p. 15)

New Mexico (nü mek′ si kō) A state in the southwestern United States. Capital, Santa Fe. (p. 15)

New Siberian Islands (nü sī bîr′ ē ən ī′ ləndz) An island group in the Arctic Ocean off the northern tip of Russia. (p. 42)

New York (nü yôrk′) A state in the eastern United States. Capital, Albany. (p. 15)

New Zealand (nü zē′ lənd) An island country in the southern Pacific Ocean, east of Australia. Capital, Wellington. (p. 71)

Niagara Falls (nī ag′ rə fôlz) A waterfall on the Niagara River, between the United States and Canada. (p. 22)

Niamey (nyä mä′) The capital and largest city of Niger; 13°N, 2°E. (p. 57)

Nicaragua (nik ə rä′ gwə) The largest country of Central America. Capital, Managua. (p. 35)

Nicosia (nik ə sē′ ə) The capital of Cyprus; 35°N, 33°E. (p. 51)

Niger (nī′ jər) A country in western Africa. Capital, Niamey. (p. 57)

Nigeria (nī jîr′ ē ə) A country in western Africa, on the Gulf of Guinea. Capital, Abuja. (p. 57)

Niger River (nī′ jər riv′ ər) A river flowing from western Africa into the Gulf of Guinea. Length, 2,600 miles (4,183 km). (p. 56)

Nile River (nīl riv′ ər) The world's longest river, flowing from east-central Africa north into the Mediterranean Sea. Length, 4,100 miles (6,560 km). (p. 50)

Niue (nē ü′ ā) An island in the southern Pacific Ocean, a possession of New Zealand. (p. 71)

Norfolk Island (nôr fək′ ī′ lənd) An Australian island in the southern Pacific Ocean. (p. 70)

North America (nôrth ə mer′ ik ə) The world's third-largest continent, lying between the Pacific and Atlantic oceans. (p. 2)

North Carolina (nôrth kar ə lī′ nə) A state in the southeastern United States. Capital, Raleigh. (p. 15)

North China Plain (nôrth chī′ nə plān) A large, fertile plain lying north of the Qin Mountains in eastern China. (p. 64)

North Dakota (nôrth də kō′ tə) A state in the north-central United States. Capital, Bismarck. (p. 15)

Northern Mariana Islands (nôr′ thern mär ē an′ ə ī′ ləndz) A group of 16 islands in the western Pacific Ocean, administered by the United States. Capital, Saipan. (p. 71)

North Pole (nôrth pōl) The northernmost point on the earth; the northern end of the earth's axis, at 90°N. (p. 42)

North Sea (nôrth sē) A large arm of the Atlantic Ocean, between Great Britain and mainland Europe. (p. 42)

Norway (nôr′ wā) A country in northern Europe. Capital, Oslo. (p. 43)

Nouakchott (nwäk′ shot) The capital of Mauritania; 18°N, 15°W. (p. 57)

Nuku'alofa (nü kü ə lō′ fə) The capital and chief port of Tonga; 23°S, 175°W. (p. 71)

O

Ob River (ob riv′ ər) A river in western Siberia, in Russia, flowing northwest and north into the Arctic Ocean. Length, 3,362 miles (5,379 km). (p. 42)

Ohio (ō hī′ ō) A state in the north-central United States. Capital, Columbus. (p. 15)

Ohio River (ō hī′ ō riv′ ər) A river in the east-central United States, flowing from Pennsylvania southwest into the Mississippi River. Length, 981 miles (1,578 km). (p. 14)

Oklahoma (ō klə hō′ mə) A state in the south-central United States. Capital, Oklahoma City. (p. 15)

Oklahoma City (ō klə hō′ mə sit′ ē) The capital of Oklahoma; 35°N, 97°W. (p. 15)

Olympia (ō lim′ pē ə) The capital of Washington; 47°N, 122°W. (p. 15)

Oman (ō män′) A country in Asia, located on the southeastern coast of the Arabian Peninsula. Capital, Muscat. (p. 51)

Oregon (ôr′ i gon) A state in the northwestern United States, on the Pacific Ocean. Capital, Salem. (p. 15)

Orinoco River (ôr ə nō′ kō riv′ ər) A large river in South America, flowing through Venezuela into the Atlantic Ocean. Length, 1,600 miles (2,574 km). (p. 34)

Oslo (os′ lō) The capital and principal city of Norway; 59°N, 10°E. (p. 43)

Ottawa (ot′ ə wə) The capital of Canada; 46°N, 71°W. (p. 15)

Ouagadougou (wä gə dü′ gü) The capital of Burkina Faso; 6°N, 1°W. (p. 57)

Ozark Plateau (o′ zärk pla tō′) A low, hilly area in southern Missouri, northern Arkansas, and northeastern Oklahoma. (p. 24)

P

Pacific Ocean (pə sif′ ik ō′ shən) The world's largest body of water, lying between Asia and Australia on the west and North America and South America on the east. (p. 2)

Pago Pago (päng′ gō päng′ ō) The capital of American Samoa; 14°S, 172°W. (p. 71)

Pakistan (pak′ ə stan) A country in southern Asia. Capital, Islamabad. (p. 65)

Palau (pä lou′) A group of Pacific Ocean islands administered by the United States. Capital, Koror. (p. 5)

Pampas (pam′ pəz) The grass-covered plains of South America that cover much of central Argentina and parts of Uruguay. (p. 34)

Panama (pan′ ə mä) A country in Central America, on the Isthmus of Panama. Capital, Panama. (p. 35)

Panama City (pan′ ə mä sit′ ē) The capital of Panama; 8°N, 79°W. (p. 35)

Papua New Guinea (pap′ ū ə nü gin′ ē) An island nation in the southwestern Pacific Ocean. Capital, Port Moresby. (p. 71)

Paraguay (par′ ə gwā) A country in south-central South America. Capital, Asunción. (p. 35)

Paramaribo (par ə mar′ ə bō) The capital of Suriname; 5°N, 55°W. (p. 35)

Paraná River (par ə nä′ riv′ ər) A river in South America, flowing through Brazil, Paraguay, and Argentina into the Río de la Plata. Length, 2,485 miles (3,976 km). (p. 34)

Paris (par′ is) The capital and largest city of France; 49°N, 2°E. (p. 43)

Patagonia (pat ə gō′ nē ə) A region in southern Argentina. (p. 34)

Pennsylvania (pen səl vān′ yə) A state in the eastern United States. Capital, Harrisburg. (p. 15)

Persian Gulf (pûr′ zhən gulf) A body of water located between the Arabian Peninsula and Iran. (p. 50)

Peru (pə rü′) A country on the western coast of South America. Capital, Lima. (p. 35)

Philippines (fil′ ə pēnz) An island country in the western Pacific Ocean, southeast of China. Capital, Manila. (p. 65)

Phnom Penh (pə nom′ pen) The capital and largest city of Cambodia; 11°N, 104°E. (p. 65)

Phoenix (fē′ niks) The capital of Arizona; 33°N, 112°W. (p. 15)

Pierre (pîr) The capital of South Dakota; 44°N, 100°W. (p. 15)

Plateau of Iran (pla′ tō əv i ran′) A plateau in the northeastern part of Iran. (p. 50)

Plateau of Tibet (pla tō′ əv ti bet′) A high, dry plateau in southwestern China, north of the Himalayas. (p. 64)

Platte River (plat riv′ ər) A river flowing from central Nebraska into the Missouri River. Length, 310 miles (499 km). (p. 26)

Point Barrow (point bar′ ō) A small Alaskan peninsula, the northernmost point of the United States. (p. 14)

Poland (pō′ lənd) A country in central Europe on the Baltic Sea. Capital, Warsaw. (p. 43)

Polynesia (pol ə nē′ zhə) One of the three main divisions of the Pacific Ocean Islands. (p. 71)

Port-au-Prince (pôrt ō prins′) The capital of Haiti; 18°N, 17°W. (p. 35)

Port Louis (pôrt lü′ is) The capital and largest city of Mauritius; 20°S, 57°E. (p. 5)

Port Moresby (pôrt môrz′ bē) The capital of Papua New Guinea; 9°S, 147°E. (p. 71)

Port-of-Spain (pôrt′ əv spān′) The capital of Trinidad and Tobago; 10°N, 61°W. (p. 35)

Porto-Novo (pôr′ tō nō′ vō) The capital of Benin; 7°N, 3°E. (p. 57)

Portugal (pôr′ chə gəl) A country in southwestern Europe. Capital, Lisbon. (p. 43)

a cap; ā cake; ä father; är car; âr dare; ch chain; e hen; ē me; êr clear; hw where; i bib; ī kite; ng song; o top; ō rope; ô saw; oi coin; ôr fork; ou cow; sh show; th thin; th those; u sun; ù book; ü moon; ū cute; ûr term; ə about, taken, pencil, apron, helpful; ər letter, dollar, doctor

Port-Vila (pôrt′ vē′ lə) The capital of Vanuatu; 18°S, 174°E. (p. 71)

Potomac River (pə tō′ mək riv′ ər) A river in the eastern United States, flowing through West Virginia, Virginia, and Maryland into the Chesapeake Bay. Length, 285 miles (459 km). (p. 22)

Prague (präg) The capital and largest city of the Czech Republic; 59°N, 14°E. (p. 43)

Praia (prī′ ə) The capital of Cape Verde; 15°N, 23°W. (p. 4)

Pretoria (pri tôr′ ē ə) The administrative capital of the Republic of South Africa; 25°S, 28°E. (p. 57)

Providence (prov′ i dəns) The capital and largest city of Rhode Island; 41°N, 71°W. (p. 15)

Puerto Rico (pwer′ tō rē′ kō) An island in the Greater Antilles of the West Indies. It is a commonwealth of the United States. Capital, San Juan. (p. 35)

Puget Sound (pū′ jit sound) An inlet of the Pacific Ocean, extending into the state of Washington. (p. 30)

Pyongyang (pyung′ yäng′) The capital of North Korea; 39°N, 125°E. (p. 65)

Pyrenees (pir′ ə nēz) A mountain range in the southwestern part of western Europe, extending from the Bay of Biscay to the Mediterranean Sea. (p. 42)

Q

Qatar (kä′ tər) A country in southwestern Asia, on the Arabian Peninsula. Capital, Doha. (p. 51)

Quito (kē′ tō) The capital of Ecuador; 1°S, 78°W. (p. 35)

R

Rabat (rə bät′) The capital of Morocco; 33°N, 6°W. (p. 51)

Raleigh (rô′ lē) The capital of North Carolina; 35°N, 78°W. (p. 15)

Red River (red riv′ ər) A river flowing from southwestern Oklahoma into the Mississippi River. Length, 1,270 miles (2,043 km). (p. 28)

Red Sea (red sē) A narrow sea located between the Arabian Peninsula and northeastern Africa. (p. 50)

Réunion (rē ūn′ yən) A French island off the coast of Madagascar in the Indian Ocean. (p. 57)

Reykjavik (rā′ kyə vēk) The capital and largest city of Iceland; 64°N, 21°W. (p. 43)

Rhine River (rīn riv′ ər) A river in Western Europe that flows from eastern Switzerland into the North Sea. Length, 700 miles (1,126 km). (p. 42)

Rhode Island (rōd ī′ lənd) A state in the northeastern United States. Capital, Providence. (p. 15)

Richmond (rich′ mənd) The capital of Virginia; 37°N, 77°W. (p. 15)

Riga (rē′ gə) The capital of Latvia; 56°N, 25°E. (p. 43)

Río de la Plata (rē′ ō dā lä plät′ ə) An estuary of the Paraná and Uruguay rivers, in South America. (p. 34)

Rio Grande (rē′ ō grand) A river flowing from southwestern Colorado into the Gulf of Mexico and forming the border between the United States and Mexico. Length, 1,885 miles (3,033 km). (p. 14)

Riyadh (rē yäd′) The capital of Saudi Arabia; 25°N, 47°E. (p. 51)

Rocky Mountains (rok′ ē moun′ tənz) The high, rugged mountains that stretch along the western part of North America from Alaska south to New Mexico. (p. 14)

Romania (rō mā′ nē ə) A country in southeastern Europe. Capital, Bucharest. (p. 43)

Rome (rōm) The capital of Italy; 42°N, 13°E. (p. 43)

Roseau (rō zō′) The capital of Dominica; 15°N, 61°W. (p. 35)

Rub' al-Khali (rùb al käl′ ē) A desert region in the Arabian Peninsula. Also, Great Sandy Desert. (p. 50)

Rwanda (rü än′ də) A country in east-central Africa. Capital, Kigali. (p. 57)

Russia (rush′ ə) A country in eastern Europe and northern Asia, formerly part of the Soviet Union. Capital, Moscow. (p. 43)

S

Sacramento (sak rə men′ tō) The capital of California; 39°N, 121°W. (p. 15)

Sahara (sə har′ ə) A desert in north-central Africa, the largest in the world. (p. 50)

Salem (sā′ ləm) The capital of Oregon; 44°N, 123°W. (p. 15)

Salt Lake City (sôlt lāk sit′ ē) The capital and largest city of Utah; 40°N, 111°W. (p. 15)

San'a (sä nä′) The capital of Yemen; 15°N, 44°E. (p. 51)

San Francisco Bay (san frən sis′ kō bā) An inlet of the Pacific Ocean, on the central coast of California. (p. 30)

San José (san hō zā′) The capital and largest city of Costa Rica; 9°N, 84°W. (p. 35)

San Juan (san hwän′) The capital of Puerto Rico; 18°N, 66°W. (p. 35)

San Marino (san mə rē′ nō) A small country in Europe completely surrounded by Italy. Capital, San Marino. (p. 43)

San Marino (san mə rē′ nō) The capital of San Marino; 44°N, 12°E. (p. 43)

San Salvador (san sal′ və dôr) The capital and largest city of El Salvador; 13°N, 85°W. (p. 35)

Santa Fe (san′ tə fā′) The capital of New Mexico; 35°N, 106°W. (p. 15)

Santiago (san tē ä′ gō) The capital and largest city of Chile; 34°S, 71°W. (p. 35)

Santo Domingo (san′ tō də ming′ gō) The capital and largest city of the Dominican Republic; 18°N, 69°W. (p. 35)

São Francisco River (soun frän sēs′ kù riv′ ər) A river in South America, flowing into the Atlantic Ocean. Length, 1,800 miles (2,896 km). (p. 34)

São Tomé (soun tù mä′) The capital of São Tomé and Príncipe; 0°, 7°E. (p. 57)

São Tomé and Príncipe (soun tù mä′ ənd prēn′ si pā) An island country located off the west coast of Africa, in the Gulf of Guinea. Capital, São Tomé. (p. 57)

Sarajevo (sär ə yā′ vō) The capital of Bosnia and Herzegovina; 44°N, 18°E. (p. 43)

Sardinia (sär din′ ē ə) An Italian island in the Mediterranean Sea, west of Italy. (p. 43)

Saudi Arabia (sä ü′ dē ə rā′ bē ə) A country in southwestern Asia, occupying most of the Arabian Peninsula. Capital, Riyadh. (p. 51)

Scandinavian Peninsula (skan də nā′ vē ən pə nin′ sə lə) A large peninsula in northern Europe, divided between Norway and Sweden. (p. 42)

Sea of Okhotsk (sē əv ō kotsk′) An arm of the Pacific Ocean, on the east coast of Russia. (p. 42)

Seine River (sān riv′ ər) A river flowing from eastern France northward into the English Channel. Length, 485 miles (780 km). (p. 42)

Senegal (sen i gôl′) A country in western Africa, on the Atlantic. Capital, Dakar. (p. 57)

Senegal River (sen i gôl′ riv′ ər) A river in western Africa, on the southern border of the Sahara, flowing into the Atlantic. Length, 1,000 miles (1,609 km). (p. 56)

Seoul (sōl) The capital and largest city of South Korea; 37°N, 127°E. (p. 65)

Seychelles (sā shel′) An island country in the western Indian Ocean, northeast of Madagascar. Capital, Victoria. (p. 57)

Siberia (sī bîr′ ē ə) A region of Russia, extending from the Ural Mountains to the Pacific. (p. 43)

Sicily (sis′ ə lē) An Italian island in the Mediterranean Sea, off the southwestern tip of Italy. (p. 43)

Sierra Leone (sē er′ ə lē ō′ nē) A country on the western coast of Africa. Capital, Freetown. (p. 57)

Sierra Madre (sē er′ ə mä′ drā) A mountain system in eastern and western Mexico. (p. 34)

Sierra Nevada (sē er′ ə nə vad′ ə) A mountain range in eastern California. (p. 14)

Sinai (sī′ nī) A triangular desert area in northeastern Egypt. (p. 50)

Singapore (sing′ ə pôr) A country off the southern tip of the Malay Peninsula. Capital, Singapore; 1°N, 103°E. (p. 65)

Skopje (skôp′ yā) The capital of Macedonia; 42°N, 22°W. (p. 43)

Slovenia (slō vēn′ ē ə) A country in southeastern Europe, formerly part of Yugoslavia. Capital, Ljubljana. (p. 43)

Snake River (snāk riv′ ər) A river in the northwestern United States, the principal tributary of the Columbia River. Length, 1,038 miles (1,670 km). (p. 30)

Sofia (sō′ fē ə) The capital of Bulgaria; 43°N, 23°E. (p. 43)

Solomon Islands (sol′ ə mən ī′ ləndz) An island country in the southwestern Pacific Ocean. Capital, Honiara. (p. 71)

Somalia (sō mäl′ yə) A country in eastern Africa, on the Indian Ocean and Gulf of Aden. Capital, Mogadishu. (p. 57)

South Africa, Republic of (south af′ ri kə, ri pub′ lik əv) A country in southern Africa. Administrative capital, Pretoria; judicial capital, Bloemfontein; legislative capital, Cape Town. (p. 57)

South America (south ə mer′ ik ə) The fourth-largest continent in the world, in the Western Hemisphere. (p. 2)

South Carolina (south kar ə lī′ nə) A state in the southeastern United States. Capital, Columbia. (p. 15)

South China Sea (south chī′ nə sē) A part of the Pacific Ocean, bounded by southeastern China, Vietnam, the Malay Peninsula, Borneo, and the Philippines. (p. 64)

South Dakota (south də kō′ tə) A state in the north-central United States. Capital, Pierre. (p. 15)

South Pole (south pōl) The southernmost point of the earth; 90°S. (p. 71)

South Sandwich Islands (south sand′ wich ī′ ləndz) A group of islands in the Atlantic Ocean near Antarctica. (p. 71)

Spain (spān) A country in southwestern Europe, on the Iberian Peninsula. Capital, Madrid. (p. 43)

Springfield (spring′ fēld) The capital of Illinois; 39°N, 89°W. (p. 15)

Sri Lanka (srē läng′ kə) An island country in the Indian Ocean, east of the southern tip of India. Capital, Colombo. (p. 65)

St. George's (sānt jôr′ jiz) The capital and largest city of Grenada; 12°N, 61°W. (p. 35)

St. John's (sānt jonz) The capital of Antigua and Barbuda; 17°N, 61°W. (p. 35)

St. Kitts and Nevis (sānt kits′ nē′ vis) A West Indian island nation made up of two of the Leeward Islands, St. Kitts (also called St. Christopher) and Nevis. Capital, Basseterre. (p. 35)

St. Lawrence River (sānt lôr′ əns riv′ ər) A river in North America flowing from Lake Ontario northeast into the Gulf of St. Lawrence. Length, 800 miles (1,287 km). (p. 14)

St. Lucia (sānt lü′ shə) A West Indian island nation, one of the Windward Islands. Capital, Castries. (p. 35)

St. Paul (sānt pôl′) The capital of Minnesota; 44°N, 93°W. (p. 15)

Strait of Magellan (strāt əv mə jel′ ən) A strait at the southern tip of mainland South America, linking the Atlantic and the Pacific oceans. (p. 34)

St. Vincent and the Grenadines (sānt vin′ sənt and thə gren′ ə dēnz) A West Indian island nation in the Windward Islands. Capital, Kingstown. (p. 35)

Stockholm (stok′ hōm) The capital and largest city of Sweden; 59°N, 18°E. (p. 43)

Sucre (sü′ krā) The judicial capital of Bolivia; 18°S, 65°W. (p. 35)

Sudan (sü dan′) A country in northeastern Africa. Capital, Khartoum. (p. 57)

Suez Canal (sü ez′ kə nal′) A canal in northeastern Egypt, connecting the Mediterranean and Red seas. (p. 50)

---

a **cap**; ā **cake**; ä **father**; är **car**; âr **dare**; ch **chain**; e **hen**; ē **me**; êr **clear**; hw **where**; i **bib**; ī **kite**; ng **song**; o **top**; ō **rope**; ô **saw**; oi **coin**; ôr **fork**; ou **cow**; sh **show**; th **thin**; th **those**; u **sun**; ù **book**; ü **moon**; ū **cute**; ûr **term**; ə **about**, tak**e**n, penc**i**l, apr**o**n, helpf**u**l; ər l**e**tt**er**, d**o**ll**ar**, doct**or**

Suriname (sùr′ ə näm) A country on the northeastern coast of South America. Capital, Paramaribo. (p. 35)

Susquehanna River (sus kwə han′ ə riv′ ər) A river flowing through New York, Pennsylvania, and Maryland. Length, 444 miles (710 km). (p. 22)

Suva (sü′ və) The capital of Fiji; 17°S, 168°E. (p. 71)

Swaziland (swä′ ze land) A country in southeastern Africa. Capital, Mbabane. (p. 57)

Sweden (swē′ dən) A country in northern Europe. Capital, Stockholm. (p. 43)

Switzerland (swit′ sər lənd) A mountainous country in central Europe. Capital, Bern. (p. 43)

Syria (sîr′ ē ə) A country in southwestern Asia. Capital, Damascus. (p. 51)

T

Taipei (tī′ pā′) The capital of Taiwan; 25°N, 121°E. (p. 65)

Taiwan (tī′ wän′) An island country in the western Pacific Ocean. Capital, Taipei. (p. 65)

Tajikistan (tä jik′ i stän) A country in central Asia, formerly part of the Soviet Union. Capital, Dushanbe. (p. 43)

Tallahassee (tal ə has′ ē) The capital of Florida; 30°N, 84°W. (p. 15)

Tallinn (tal′ ən) The capital of Estonia; 59°N, 25°E. (p. 43)

Tanzania (tan zə nē′ ə) A country in east-central Africa. Capitals, Dodoma and Dar es Salaam. (p. 57)

Tarawa (tə rä′ wə) The capital of Kiribati; 1°N, 174°E. (p. 71)

Tashkent (tash kent′) The capital of Uzbekistan; 41°N, 69°E. (p. 43)

Tbilisi (tə bil′ ə sē) The capital of Georgia; 42°N, 45°E. (p. 43)

Tegucigalpa (tə gü si gal′ pə) The capital of Honduras; 14°N, 87°W. (p. 35)

Tehran (te rän′) The capital and largest city of Iran; 35°N, 51°E. (p. 51)

Tennessee (ten ə sē′) A state in the southeastern United States. Capital, Nashville. (p. 15)

Texas (tek′ səs) A state in the south-central United States. Capital, Austin. (p. 15)

Thailand (tī′ land) A country in southeastern Asia. Capital, Bangkok. (p. 65)

Thimphu (tim′ pü) The capital of Bhutan; 28°N, 90°E. (p. 65)

Tibet (ti bet′) A country in southwestern China, claimed by the People's Republic of China. Capital, Lhasa. (p. 65)

Tierra del Fuego (tyer ə del fwä′ gō) An archipelago at the southern tip of South America. (p. 34)

Tigris River (tī′ gris riv′ ər) A river in southwestern Asia, flowing from eastern Turkey into the Persian Gulf. Length, 1,180 miles (1,899 km). (p. 50)

Timor Sea (tē′ môr sē) An arm of the Indian Ocean, between Indonesia and Australia. (p. 64)

Tiranë (ti rä′ nə) The capital and largest city of Albania; 41°N, 20°E. (p. 43)

Togo (tō′ gō) A country in western Africa on the Gulf of Guinea. Capital, Lomé. (p. 57)

Tokelau (tō′ kə lou) A group of three atolls administered by New Zealand, in the Pacific Ocean. (p. 71)

Tokyo (tō′ kyō) The capital and largest city of Japan; 36°N, 140°E. (p. 65)

Tonga (tong′ gə) A country consisting of islands in the southern Pacific Ocean. Capital, Nuku'alofa. (p. 71)

Topeka (tə pē′ kə) The capital of Kansas; 39°N, 35°W. (p. 15)

Trenton (tren′ tən) The capital of New Jersey; 40°N, 70°W. (p. 15)

Trinidad and Tobago (trin′ i dad ənd tə bā′ gō) A country consisting of the West Indian islands of Trinidad and Tobago. Capital, Port-of-Spain. (p. 35)

Tripoli (trip′ ə lē) The capital and largest city of Libya; 32°N, 13°E. (p. 51)

Tunis (tü′nis) The capital and largest city of Tunisia; 37°N, 10°E. (p. 51)

Tunisia (tü nē′ zhə) A country on the northern coast of Africa, on the Mediterranean Sea. Capital, Tunis. (p. 51)

Turkey (tûr′ kē) A country in western Asia and southeastern Europe. Capital, Ankara. (p. 51)

Turkmenistan (tûrk men′ i stän) A country in central Asia, formerly part of the Soviet Union. Capital, Ashkhabad. (p. 43)

Tuvalu (tù vä′ lü) An island country in the central Pacific Ocean. Capital, Funafuti. (p. 71)

U

Uganda (ū gan′ də) A country in east-central Africa. Capital, Kampala. (p. 57)

Ukraine (ū krän′) A country in eastern Europe, formerly part of the Soviet Union. Capital, Kiev. (p. 43)

Ulaanbaatar (ü′ län bä′ tôr) The capital and largest city of Mongolia; 47°N, 107°E. (p. 65)

United Arab Emirates (ū nī′ tid ar′ əb em′ ər its) A country composed of seven sheikdoms on the east-central coast of the Arabian Peninsula. Capital, Abu Dhabi. (p. 51)

United Kingdom (ū nī′ tid king′ dəm) A country in Europe, composed of England, Scotland, Wales, and Northern Ireland. Capital, London. (p. 43)

United States (ū nī′ tid stāts) A country mainly in North America, consisting of 50 states. Capital, Washington, D.C. (p. 15)

Ural Mountains (yùr′ əl moun′ tənz) A mountain system extending north to south in the east-central Soviet Union, forming part of the traditional boundary between Europe and Asia. (p. 42)

Uruguay (yùr′ ə gwā) A country on the southeastern coast of South America. Capital, Montevideo. (p. 35)

Uruguay River (yùr′ ə gwā riv′ ər) A river in southeastern South America, flowing into the Río de la Plata. Length, 1,000 miles (1,609 km). (p. 34)

Utah (u′ tô) A state in the western United States. Capital, Salt Lake City. (p. 15)

Uzbekistan (uz bek′ i stän) A country in central Asia, formerly part of the Soviet Union. Capital, Tashkent. (p. 43)

V

Vaduz (vä düts′) The capital of Liechtenstein; 47°N, 9°E. (p. 43)

Valletta (və let′ ə) The capital of Malta; 35°N, 14°E. (p. 43)

Vanuatu (van ü ä′ tü) A country in the southwestern Pacific Ocean. Capital, Port-Vila. (p. 71)

Vatican City (vat′ i kən sit′ ē) An independent state located within Rome. Seat of the Roman Catholic Church; 42°N, 12°E. (p. 43)

Venezuela (ven ə zwā′ lə) A country in South America, on the Caribbean Sea. Capital, Caracas. (p. 35)

Verkhoyansk Mountains (vyer kə yansk′ moun′ tənz) A mountain range in the northeastern part of Russia, south of the Arctic Ocean. (p. 42)

Vermont (vər mont′) A state in the northeastern United States. Capital, Montpelier. (p. 15)

Victoria (vik tôr′ ē ə) The capital of Seychelles; 6°S, 54°E. (p. 57)

Vienna (vē en′ ə) The capital and largest city of Austria; 48°N, 16°E. (p. 43)

Vientiane (vyen tyän′) The capital and largest city of Laos; 18°N, 103°E. (p. 65)

Vietnam (vē et näm′) A country in southeastern Asia. Capital, Hanoi. (p. 65)

Vilnius (vil′ nē əs) The capital of Lithuania; 55°N, 25°E. (p. 43)

Vinson Massif (vint′ sən ma sēf′) The sixth-highest mountain in the world, located in Antarctica. Height, 16,864 feet (5,140 m). (p. 71)

Virginia (vər jin′ yə) A state in the eastern United States. Capital, Richmond. (p. 15)

Virgin Islands (vûr′ jin ī′ ləndz) An island group of the Caribbean. It is divided politically between the United States and Great Britain. (p. 35)

Volga River (vol′ gə riv′ ər) A river in western Russia. Length, 2,194 miles (3,530 km). (p. 42)

W

Wake Island (wāk ī′ lənd) An atoll in the Pacific Ocean, administered by the United States. (p. 5)

Warsaw (wôr′ sô) The capital and largest city of Poland; 52°N, 21°E. (p. 43)

Washington (wô′ shing tən) A state in the northwestern United States. Capital, Olympia. (p. 15)

Washington, D.C. (wô′ shing tən dē sē) The capital of the United States. It is also known as the District of Columbia; 38°N, 77°W. (p. 15)

Wellington (wel′ ing tən) The capital of New Zealand; 41°S, 174°E. (p. 71)

Western Sahara (wes′ tûrn sə har′ ə) A territory on the northwestern coast of Africa, claimed by Morocco. Capital, El Aaiún. (p. 51)

Western Samoa (wes′ tûrn sə mō′ ə) An island country in the southern Pacific Ocean, east of Australia, consisting of the western islands of Samoa. Capital, Apia. (p. 71)

West Virginia (west vər jin′ yə) A state in the eastern United States. Capital, Charleston. (p. 15)

Windhoek (vint′ hük) The capital of Namibia; 22°S, 17°E. (p. 57)

Wisconsin (wis kon′ sin) A state in the north-central United States. Capital, Madison. (p. 15)

Wrangel Island (rang′ gəl ī′ lənd) An island off the coast of Russia, in the Arctic Ocean. (p. 42)

Wyoming (wī ō′ ming) A state in the western United States. Capital, Cheyenne. (p. 15)

Y

Yangon (yan′ gôn′) The capital of Myanmar (Burma), formerly called Rangoon; 16°N, 96°E. (p. 65)

Yaoundé (yä ün dā′) The capital of Cameroon; 4°N, 11°E. (p. 57)

Yaren (yâr′ ən) The capital of Nauru; 0°, 168°E. (p. 71)

Yellow Sea (yel′ ō sē) A shallow arm of the Pacific Ocean, between northeastern China and North Korea and South Korea. (p. 64)

Yemen (yem′ ən) A country in the southwestern part of the Arabian Peninsula, on the Red Sea. Capital, San'a. (p. 51)

Yerevan (yer ə vän′) The capital of Armenia; 40°N, 45°E. (p. 43)

Yucatán (ü kə tan′) A peninsula between the Gulf of Mexico and the Caribbean Sea. (p. 34)

Yugoslavia (ü gō slä′ vē ə) A country in southeastern Europe. Capital, Belgrade. (p. 43)

Z

Zagreb (zäg′ reb) The capital of Croatia; 45°N, 16°W. (p. 43)

Zagros Mountains (zag′ rəs moun′ tənz) A mountain range extending along the borders of Iran and Iraq. (p. 50)

Zaire (zä îr′) A country in central Africa. Capital, Kinshasa. (p. 57)

Zambia (zam′ bē ə) A country in south-central Africa. Capital, Lusaka. (p. 57)

Zanzibar (zan′ zə bär) An island in the Indian Ocean, off the eastern coast of Africa, part of Tanzania. (p. 56)

Zimbabwe (zim bäb′ wē) A country in south-central Africa. Capital, Harare. (p. 57)

---

a cap; ā cake; ä father; är car; âr dare; ch chain; e hen; ē me; êr clear; hw where; i bib; ī kite; ng song; o top; ō rope; ô saw; oi coin; ôr fork; ou cow; sh show; th thin; <u>th</u> those; u sun; ù book; ü moon; ū cute; ûr term; ə about, taken, pencil, apron, helpful; ər letter, dollar, doctor

PHOTOGRAPHY CREDITS

ILLUSTRATION CREDITS